·   P L A T O   ·

S Y M P O S I U M   A N D
P H A E D R U S

It has been said that, after the Bible, Plato's
dialogues are the most influential books in
Western culture. Of these, the *Symposium* is
by far the most delightful and accessible,
requiring no special knowledge of philosophy or Greek society. Describing a party
in the Athens of the fifth century BC, this
short and deceptively unassuming book
introduces profound ideas about the nature
of love in the guise of convivial after-dinner
conversation. Published together with the
Symposium is *Phaedrus*, in which Plato dis-
cusses the place of eloquence in expounding
truth. Socrates plays the leading role in both
dialogues, by turns arguing, joking, and
teasing his followers into understanding
ideas that have remained central to Western
thought ever since.

EVERYMAN'S LIBRARY

EVERYMAN,
I WILL GO WITH THEE,
AND BE THY GUIDE,
IN THY MOST NEED
TO GO BY THY SIDE

PLATO

Symposium and Phaedrus

Translated by Tom Griffith
with an Introduction by R. B. Rutherford

EVERYMAN'S LIBRARY

Alfred A. Knopf New York Toronto

194

THIS IS A BORZOI BOOK

PUBLISHED BY ALFRED A. KNOPF, INC.

Translation of *Symposium* © University of California Press, 1989
Translation of *Phaedrus* © Tom Griffith, 2000

These translations first included in Everyman's Library 2000

Introduction, Bibliography, and Chronology Copyright © 2000
by Everyman Publishers plc
Typography by Peter B. Willberg

ISBN 0-375-41174-7

Book Design by Barbara de Wilde and Carol Devine Carson

Typeset in the UK by AccComputing, Castle Cary, Somerset

Printed and bound in Germany
by Graphischer Grossbetrieb Pössneck GmbH

PLATO

CONTENTS

———

INTRODUCTION

This volume contains translations of two of the most readable and enjoyable of Plato's dramatic dialogues: the *Symposium* (the name means 'The Drinking Party') and the *Phaedrus* (named after one of the two participants in the work). Like almost all of his works, they have as their central character the figure of Socrates, Plato's remarkable teacher, one of the most eccentric and endearing figures in classical literature. There are many other works by Plato, covering a bewildering range of topics, from practical ethics to theory of knowledge, from the merits of different political systems to the defects of traditional education. Although Plato is nowadays automatically cast as a philosopher, his writings touch on many topics which are marginal to most later thinkers: fields such as religion, aesthetics, the structure of society, the art of rhetoric. The two dialogues which are presented here form a natural pair, as both are concerned with erotic love, more specifically love between males.

The openness with which the theme is discussed has sometimes aroused strong antagonism in periods which frowned on homosexuality: sometimes the texts have been cut or bowdlerized, and some translators have even tried to give the impression that Plato was in fact writing about heterosexuality. In our time, neither dialogue is likely to evoke the same degree of alarm: but it is important to recognize that homosexuality, and love itself, are not absolute or timeless concepts: rather, they vary in different periods and different cultures. Plato was writing in the first half of the fourth century BC, in Athens, as a well-born and well-educated citizen of a society very different from any that exists today: his concerns and his assumptions, on both the public and the private level, were different from ours. But to say that they were different is not to say that they are inaccessible. It is perfectly possible to read and enjoy both these works without knowing much about their background; some knowledge of the context, however, will probably assist the reader, and this short introduction is intended to provide that assistance. What follows covers three main topics. First, I describe the historical context and the career of Socrates, the 'hero' of Plato's work; second, I discuss Plato's use of Socrates as a character and of the dialogue form; finally, I offer some comments on the subject matter of the dialogues and their handling of the theme of love.

*

The lifetime of the Athenian Socrates coincided with perhaps the most remarkable period of classical Greek history, particularly the history of Athenian democracy and its literary and artistic achievements. Born in 469 BC, Socrates grew to adulthood in the period of the radical democracy, the most advanced that had existed in the world up to that time, in which all adult male citizens were entitled to play a role in the government of Athens. Although even in a society small by modern standards some degree of representative government was necessary, any decision of the representative council (a body appointed by lot, which normally met daily) had to be ratified by the citizen body gathered in an assembly meeting. In this period Athens reached its peak in military and political power, gradually transforming the league of states which had banded together to resist the Persian invasions into an empire governed by Athens and paying tribute to it. Under the strong leadership of the statesman Pericles, Athens embarked on a lengthy war (usually known as the Peloponnesian war) against its chief rival Sparta rather than restore autonomy to its allies or accept any other reduction of its power. This conflict, begun in 431, lasted with intervals of truce till 404, when Athens was defeated by Sparta and was temporarily forced to submit to a puppet government imposed by Sparta, later known as 'the Thirty Tyrants'. The Peloponnesian war, recognized already at the time as spectacularly long and destructive, was chronicled by the great historian Thucydides in a narrative which remains central to our understanding of the age. Thucydides never mentions Socrates, but the latter participated in some of the campaigns which the historian described, and more generally, the picture we get from Thucydides of the ideological and intellectual conditions of the time provides invaluable background for the study of Plato.

The second half of the fifth century BC was as notable for its cultural as for its political legacy. The prosperity of Athens as leader of the Hellenic alliance led to the construction of the architectural monuments which still dominate the highest part of Athens today: the Parthenon was begun in 447, the Propylaea or great gateway which leads on to the Acropolis in 437. These and other works were undertaken on the proposals of Pericles, whose friend Pheidias, one of the greatest sculptors of antiquity, oversaw the building programme. Socrates in his earliest years might have just seen the last plays of the tragedian Aeschylus, but would have been far more familiar with the developing work of the equally gifted dramatists Sophocles and Euripides. He seems to have been on friendly terms with the comic poet Aristophanes, who appears as a member of the dinner party recalled in the *Symposium*: there were no bad feelings, it seems, about the parodic treatment of Socrates' teaching which Aristophanes had presented a few years earlier in his *Clouds* (423 BC: a phrase is quoted by Alcibiades at *Symp.* 221b). Much of the work of these writers survives today and is still admired; equal heights, apparently, were reached by the orators, though no fifth-century political oratory has been preserved. Socrates and his peers have heard and admired Pericles' orations (*Symp.* 215e, *Ph.* 270a), and we shall see that Socrates himself takes a keen interest in the theory and practice of rhetoric.

All of the figures mentioned so far were Athenian-born. But many others visited Athens to admire or gain advantage from its power and wealth. Among the intellectuals who gravitated to this centre of empire we should note especially the so-called sophists, teachers of various kinds, of whom Protagoras and Gorgias are the best-known. Some of these men were older than Socrates and may well have influenced him, but in Plato's works they are generally treated with disapproval, or at best irony. They were notable thinkers in their own right, who taught a wide range of subjects, but most if not all sophists were especially associated in the popular mind with the teaching of skill in rhetoric. The power of speech was of fundamental importance in Athens for anyone wishing to embark on a political career, for it was through oratory and public debate that the politician must persuade the assembly, defend himself against abuse or attacks, counter the opposing view of his rivals. Plato's dialogues show us many ambitious young men who seek to learn the secrets of success in public life, and who believe that they can do so best by studying with the sophists. In several works he presents Socrates engaged in sceptical argument with both the teachers and the pupils: in the *Protagoras*, which shows Socrates arguing against the sophist of that name, it is clear that both Protagoras' claims to expertise and the aims of his teaching are being called into question.

Socrates himself was not an ambitious man, and indeed avoided involvement in public affairs. Of his wife and sons we know little; the son of a stone-mason, he seems to have been a poor man throughout his life, though he is represented in Plato as being on easy terms with much wealthier and more distinguished figures. Others were drawn to him by his way of talking, his interest in examining and questioning assumptions which most people took for granted. His quick eye for the weaknesses in an argument, and his moral seriousness, earned him a reputation for wisdom, though he himself was quick to deny that he had any special knowledge: in one memorable passage, Plato makes him declare that the only wisdom he possesses is that, unlike others, he is aware of his own ignorance (*Apology* 23).

Although disinclined to participate in politics, he could not avoid the obligatory military service imposed on able-bodied citizens, and we hear in the *Symposium* of his service in two campaigns in the earlier part of the war against Sparta and its allies. Alcibiades praises him as a courageous but prudent soldier, though we are also given glimpses of the oddities of his behaviour, some of which annoyed the other troops (*Symp.* 219e–21b). At a later date he seems to have been a member of the council, and took a strong line in opposition to a proposal for mass execution of a number of unsuccessful generals (*Apology* 32a–b, Xenophon, *Hellenica* i.7.15), though he failed to carry the day. His moral courage was also shown in the period when the Thirty were in control of Athens after the end of the war. Seeking to involve as many citizens as possible in their crimes, the Thirty ordered Socrates to go and arrest an innocent man whose property they were eager to appropriate. He went home and ignored the order, and might well have suffered for this had the Thirty not swiftly fallen from power (*Apology* 32c–d).

Socrates was clearly an eccentric and unusual citizen – in appearance, too, he was peculiar, as Alcibiades mischievously comments (*Symp.* 215a–c) – but only in the last years of his life does a belief seem to have arisen that he was dangerous. In 399 BC three prosecutors brought charges against him for corrupting the young through his teaching, and believing in strange gods while disbelieving in the traditional gods of Athenian religion. We may well imagine that in the moody and acrimonious atmosphere of defeated Athens there were some who ascribed the city's failures to a neglect of religious practice, and scapegoats were perhaps being sought. But other factors seem to have been relevant. First, over the years Socrates' arguments and quibbling with all those he met had built up a considerable hostility towards him, especially as his young friends were seen to be imitating his sceptical style of questioning. Second, if we can believe that some of the lines of argument Socrates adopts in Plato are authentic, then he may have been seen as hostile to democracy. Third, his long-term association with controversial figures such as the ambitious but unscrupulous Alcibiades, or the oligarchs Critias and Charmides, may have led others to suppose that he endorsed or even encouraged their actions. At all events, a jury of Athenians convicted Socrates on the charges as stated, and condemned him to death. After a period in prison, during which he continued to engage in lively discussions with his friends, he took the poisonous hemlock which Athenian law prescribed for those condemned on capital charges.

It is not surprising that those who knew Socrates well were outraged by this sequence of events, and a considerable body of literature seems swiftly to have been put in circulation in subsequent years, much of it concerned to defend Socrates and to preserve his memory. The defensive aspect is most explicit in Xenophon's work 'Recollections of Socrates', often called by the Latin title *Memorabilia*. Several of Plato's works are directly concerned with the prelude to the master's death: the *Apology* offers a literary version of Socrates' own defence-speech at his trial; the *Crito* shows him in prison, conversing with a friend and resisting advice to escape to exile in another city: with typical lack of self-interest, he argued that if the laws of Athens had condemned him, it was his duty, as a citizen, to accept this fate. Finally, Plato's *Phaedo* movingly commemorates his final hours of life. But other works are connected more obliquely with the trial and charges: for instance, it is arguable that the *Symposium* is partly intended to present a true picture of the relationship between Socrates and Alcibiades, according to which the former is not Alcibiades' corrupter but a good influence which the young man acknowledges as such but eventually abandons.

Socrates himself wrote nothing, and indeed in the *Phaedrus* he is represented as disapproving of writing (274b–8e). Our knowledge of him is entirely dependent on the writings of others, most notably Plato and Xenophon. Both of these were much younger men: Plato, born in 427, could have encountered Socrates only in his last years, when the latter was already in his sixties. The influence was evidently formative. Apart from the *Apology*, all Plato's works are composed in dialogue form, and all but the last include Socrates as a character. Since Plato does not include himself as a character in his dialogues, and never prefaces them with a statement of his aims or authorial prologue, and since little contemporary evidence tells us much about Plato's life and thought beyond what we can deduce from the dialogues, the problem of interpreting the relationship between Plato and Socrates, author and character, pupil and teacher, is extremely complicated and probably insoluble. A common view is that Plato began by reproducing the style of Socrates' conversation and the substance of his teachings, but gradually moved beyond them to present his own ideas through Socrates' lips; many other positions, however, are possible. The problem is aggravated by the uncertain chronology of Plato's works, many of which cannot be dated even approximately. Statistical study of Plato's style and language has led scholars to divide the dialogues into groups, designated early, middle and late. The *Symposium* can be placed after 385 BC because of an anachronistic historical reference to an event of that year (*Symp.* 193a, with note). Both the *Symposium* and the *Phaedrus* probably fall in Plato's 'middle period', the late 380s or 370s, but more exact dating is virtually impossible. It is usually thought that the *Symposium* is the earlier work, and that is assumed here.

Socrates evidently did not 'teach' in the sense of signing people up for a course and going through it from start to finish: rather, he talked willingly with anyone he met, and explored ideas rather than voicing dogma. In view of this, and also the absence of written statements from Socrates himself about his opinions, it is unlikely that even his closest friends would have been able to expound a coherent body of 'Socratic doctrine'. It is in fact doubtful that that was ever Plato's aim. The choice of dialogue form seems crucial, and suggests that Plato was at least as concerned to record the personality, the conversational style, the argumentative method, of his mentor. Dialogue includes a diversity of characters, and allows the exchange and development of different views; in the dialogues conventionally labelled 'early', we may wish to see Socrates as the 'hero' or main character, but others besides him say things that are worth considering, and his arguments do not always convince his companions or the reader. Dialogue is not only a lively dramatic device, but has intellectual advantages. Since Plato does not intervene in his own voice to tell the reader what to think, the reader has to do more of the work for him/herself. Some dialogues end with the question unresolved, or opposing views unreconciled. Philosophic enquiry is represented as a continuing search, not a matter of memorizing an established set of principles.

We should also accept that some of the interest of Platonic dialogue, for both author and reader, is literary. In ancient times there were stories that Plato had attempted to write poetry, or specifically tragedy, but burned these misguided efforts after meeting Socrates and turning to philosophy. Though probably fiction, these anecdotes are a way of explaining an undeniable fact, that Plato's works are often dramatic – the dialogues include vivid scene-setting, varied

characters who talk in different styles, unexpected develop-
ments (as when the drunken Alcibiades crashes the party in
the *Symposium*). Moreover, the stylistic texture of his work is
extraordinarily rich, as comes through even in translation. The
poetic speech of Agathon, the marvellous mysticism of the
finale to Diotima's exposition, are the work of a lover of words
and language. In Plato's time literature and philosophy had
not been clearly differentiated – the very term 'philosophy'
may even be a Platonic coinage. Although in the *Republic* Plato
makes Socrates criticize and censor literature, and has him
declare that 'there is an ancient quarrel between philosophy
and poetry' (607b–c), the *Symposium* and the *Phaedrus* show how
the two could be creatively united: here, indeed, the *littérateur*
may be said to have the upper hand.

It is time to take a closer look at the two dialogues translated
in this volume. They are more ambitious, but less easy to
summarize, than some of the short, early dialogues. In works
such as the *Laches* and the *Euthyphro* Plato has Socrates and
his companions examine a particular moral concept, such as
courage or piety, in an effort to reach a definition of that
concept which will stand up to scrutiny. The delightful inform-
ality and badinage are as prominent as in the dialogues in this
volume, but in these other works there is a clear agenda; often,
however, a dialogue ends with an admission that they have not
yet solved the problem, and must try again another time. In
the *Symposium*, rather than following an informal conversational line, the dialogue shows the influence of more formal
rhetoric, particularly the encomium or speech of praise,
already a well-established rhetorical genre (177b–c). The discussion is couched in longer speeches: each speaker seeks to
provide not a definition but an encomium, an oration in praise
of, Love, whether conceived as a divine power or as the
emotion of love or the institution or social process of falling in
love and conducting a relationship. The dialogue reaches a
climax with Socrates' speech, which outclasses the others in
length and eloquence; but after he has finished, there is a
further speech from a new arrival, Alcibiades, who sings
the praises not of Love but of his own beloved Socrates, revealing much about both of them in the process. Although there is

some incidental argumentative sparring over particular propositions, especially between Socrates and his host Agathon, the *Symposium* does not reach any obvious philosophical conclusions.

The *Phaedrus* is a work which deals with some of the same themes in a completely different way. Even its form is distinct: whereas the *Symposium* involved a narrator, Apollodorus, who passes on to a friend an account of the occasion, selecting and quoting from a wide variety of participants, the *Phaedrus* is in purely dramatic form, with the entire work consisting of direct speech between only two characters, Socrates and his young friend Phaedrus. Since Phaedrus was also present in the *Symposium*, and played a decisive part in suggesting the subject for the speeches, he provides a link between the two works; other connections include the reappearance of speech-making (Phaedrus has just come from a perfomance by the distinguished orator Lysias), and speeches on the theme of love. Both dialogues include a magnificent and stylistically extravagant speech by Socrates which in some sense gives the 'truth' about love, a subject on which he claims to be something of an expert; but in neither case can we see Socrates' main speech as providing all the 'answers' or as the *raison d'être* of the dialogue. In the *Symposium* Socrates' speech is followed and in a way countered by Alcibiades' much more passionate and emotional praise of Socrates; in the *Phaedrus* the conversation turns to other topics, and the speech is referred to only casually, without further examination of its content. It is even possible to see the subject of love in that work as incidental, secondary to the critique of contemporary rhetoric.

Nevertheless, both dialogues have traditionally and rightly been seen as saying something novel and important about the lover's experience. The term 'Platonic love' is a cliché, though generally misunderstood: for Plato, the highest form of love involves transcending rather than merely refraining from the physical experience. 'Love' here means the love between men, and the love of women is treated as a lesser affair. It is a reasonable enough guess that this reflects Plato's own preferences, but it also arises from the social and educational situation in classical Athens. Women do not participate in Plato's dialogues. Although the priestess Diotima is cited as Socrates' authority in his speech in the *Symposium*, she may well be a fictional figure, and is in any case not present at the drinking-party. Similarly in the *Phaedo*, Socrates' wife is sent away before the final moments, and the philosopher dies with his male intimates, not with his family. While many texts also suggest that happy marriages existed, and some women were later admitted to Plato's school, the Academy, in the Platonic dialogues, it is assumed that serious intellectual and emotional interchange will be between men. This does not, however, signify a homosexual society or class of society: it is rather that men regularly engaged in relationships, flirtatious or long-standing, with other men, prior to or outside marriage. One regular pattern was for an older and a younger man to enjoy such a relationship for a number of years: a distinction was drawn between the 'lover' (*erastes*) and the 'beloved' (*eromenos*), the younger man playing the latter role. The lover was expected to pursue and persist in 'wooing' the beloved, while the beloved should not yield his favours too readily, still less make it appear that he was doing so for any mercenary motives. Once established, such a liaison may sometimes have continued as a lasting homosexual relationship: Pausanias and Agathon are one such case, whose special affinity is remarked upon by Aristophanes in the *Symposium* (193b–c). But in most cases the older man would move on, and the younger man would grow up to be an *erastes* in his turn with his juniors.

This background helps us understand much that is said in both dialogues; it also allows for much humour and ironic wit in the handling of the Socrates–Alcibiades relationship. Socrates in a number of the dialogues makes out that he is highly susceptible to the good looks of young men, and more specifically that he is infatuated with Alcibiades, an extremely handsome, well-born and gifted young Athenian. Since he himself is the older man (and unprepossessing in appearance), it seems obvious that he must be the pursuer, the lover, and a fairly unattractive one at that. But in fact, as Alcibiades reveals, he has been so fascinated by Socrates' conversation and wisdom that he himself has virtually turned into the pursuer, the desperate wooer (217b–c), only to find that Socrates spurns his

INTRODUCTION

increasingly shameless advances and treats his protestations
with ironic indifference (218–19). This richly amusing narrative
also makes a moral point: that Socrates' self-discipline extends
to his emotions, that he is composed and in command of
himself where Alcibiades is unrestrained and self-indulgent;
moreover, it suggests that Socrates has himself advanced
a considerable way along the path that his main speech
describes, a path leading to a higher and more sublime conception of love as something which transcends mere physical desire
for beauty as found in the human body, something which
aspires to *beauty itself*.

To understand what is meant here it is necessary to draw
on dialogues other than these two, though we must also be
cautious in assuming that a single consistent Platonic philosophy can be constructed by combining elements from various
works of Plato. Among the themes which recur most frequently
in dialogues of the early to middle period, and which receive
special emphasis through Socrates' words, are the superiority
of the human soul (which is immortal) to the body and of virtue
to pleasure or self-indulgence. Plato's presentation of the moral
life lays stress on the cultivation of the soul and on self-control
and self-knowledge as practised by Socrates. It seems often to
be assumed that virtuous action follows on insight or knowledge of what virtue is: in a formulation which may go back to
the original Socrates, 'virtue is knowledge'. Moreover, Plato
frequently refers to the need for knowledge to go beyond par-
ticulars: rather than defining courage by listing a number of
courageous actions, Socrates is concerned to find out what
courage is in itself. In Plato, this definitional tactic is related
to a metaphysical assumption: that in some sense courage does
exist as an entity, real and knowable, perhaps on some higher
plane; and the same goes for the other virtues and abstract
qualities, including beauty. This is the so-called Theory of
Forms, expounded most fully in the *Phaedo* and the *Republic*,
according to which individual agents and actions partake of
the Form of courage or beauty, but only partially, and always
fall short of the full and perfect condition which belongs only
to the Form itself. The relation of these Forms to the gods, in
whom Socrates and Plato plainly believed though conceiving

them in different terms from the average Greek, is not altogether clear, but full knowledge of the Forms is associated with
the gods, and to apprehend them fully would be as close to a
godlike state as man can attain.

In the myth which Socrates tells in his longest speech in the
Phaedrus, these and other theories are combined in a dazzling
symbolic narrative describing the flight of the souls of gods
and men through the cosmos, where the absolute reality of the
Forms can be experienced, and the ways in which a soul loses
its wings, growing too closely attached to the corporeal life of
the world we live in; but through the recognition of beauty in
a beloved object the wings can be made to grow once more.
Imagery of division in the soul (visualized as a chariot with
driver and two horses), ideas of reincarnation in different
animal and human forms, correspondences between different
types of soul and different deities, concepts of purity and
immortality, divine inspiration and human aspiration to the
divine, are mingled in an extraordinary vision which is easier
to admire as a prose-poem than to paraphrase in doctrinal
terms. Later ancient writers found the extravagance of the
Phaedrus excessive; taking a hint from Socrates' own comments
on his efforts (238d, 241e), they labelled the style 'dithyrambic',
that is, more suited to the wild versification of songs in honour
of the wine-god Bacchus than to the sobriety of prose. The
modern reader, less handicapped by an over-rigid conception
of stylistic proprieties, may prefer to relish the imaginative
splendour of Plato's most poetic work. Nor, perhaps, need we
struggle too hard to paraphrase Socrates' 'teachings' about
love in prosaic terms. It is clear that both the *Symposium* and
the *Phaedrus* allude to and embroider on ideas which are
explained in more expository form elsewhere: the quest of the
soul for moral perfection, the superiority of the moral and
metaphysical world to the physical, the importance of moral
choice in life – but to try to chain down every detail and
interpret these speeches as strict allegories or according to a
very precise system is surely a mistake.

Love is one subject that seems important to both dialogues,
but as already explained, it is perhaps less important in the
Phaedrus. The other theme central to the latter is rhetoric, its

powers, perils and limitations. This is present in the *Symposium* but plays a less conspicuous role: there are passing jibes at the fashion for paradoxical praise of trivial subjects, and Agathon is teased for his elegant but vacuous style of speaking, which recalls the manner of the sophist Gorgias (177b, 198a). Even here, however, the eloquence of Socrates is emphasized, and so is the way in which (unlike that of the other speakers), it has been applied to a morally worthy purpose, the expression of truth rather than well-turned-out lies (198d–e), and the correction of moral error (in his rebukes to Alcibiades). In the *Phaedrus* much more is said about contemporary oratory and its defects. Phaedrus has come fresh from a recitation by Lysias, whose speech he admires far beyond its deserts; at the end of the dialogue Socrates comments on the talents of the young Isocrates, another practitioner of the art; and in much of the second half of the work, Socrates is concerned to expose the deficiencies of rhetoric, most obviously in the passage where he makes fun of the technical terms used by the sophists and other writers of handbooks (266d–7e).

Socrates in general is represented by Plato as an opponent of rhetoric. He is distrustful of the effect of deceptive speeches on large audiences, disapproves of the way in which political speakers appeal to the emotions rather than the intellect, and believes that they do not possess the knowledge of morality that alone could justify their authority. Often, indeed, as in the lawcourts, truth must be sacrificed to plausibility: in the orator's eyes it is more important to win than to stick to the truth, but Socrates would never accept this. Politics, however, are on the fringes of this dialogue, though elsewhere, in the *Gorgias*, Socrates confronts political oratory and the ambition of the orator head on. In the *Phaedrus*, set in a country spot remote from the political arena, Socrates and Phaedrus are concerned to evaluate the recent performance of Lysias, but the speech itself is also detached from politics. Lysias has argued the paradoxical case that a boy should yield his erotic favours to one who does not love him rather than one who does. If the real Lysias did indeed deliver a speech on this theme, it was presumably no more than an ingenious game; but Socrates takes it seriously, and uses the speech as a springboard for two speeches of his own, which in different ways reveal that of Lysias as artistically inept, morally despicable, and founded on a low opinion of human nature and a shallow conception of the nature of passionate love. In the later part of the dialogue Socrates goes on to hint at the possibility of a better form of rhetoric, one which would be founded on philosophic insight (261a) and on a deep understanding of the psychology of the addressee (270c–72b, etc.). This is indeed what he himself has been practising throughout his conversation with Phaedrus. The art of the lover and of the true orator are akin, for the true orator will care for and look after the interests of his audience. The two roles are combined in the Socrates of the *Phaedrus*.

Behind Socrates stands Plato, himself a gifted artist with words. Like his mentor, he viewed oratory as practised in assembly and courts with deep suspicion: after all, it was deceptive and malicious oratory that had secured Socrates' condemnation by a popular jury. As a citizen of Athens in the late fifth and early fourth centuries, Plato would have witnessed many other occasions on which the art of persuasion had led to destructive or damaging decisions. But Plato was also a teacher – more so than Socrates, who probably asked questions more than answering them. Plato was indeed the founder and head of a school, the Academy, established probably in the 380s: however different this may have been from modern educational institutions, it must have involved some form of instruction. No teacher can be indifferent to the techniques of persuasion, but rhetoric as taught in the handbooks seemed to Plato morally dubious and psychologically inadequate. When Socrates at the end of the *Phaedrus* (278e–9b) alludes to Isocrates as a young man of exceptional promise, more gifted than Lysias and his like, this is more relevant to Plato in the 370s than to Socrates before 399, for Isocrates had by then achieved considerable distinction as a teacher and essayist, a rival to Plato, who even appropriated the title of 'philosophy' for his own educational programme. The patronizing and ironic praise in the *Phaedrus* puts Isocrates in his place before his career is even under way. The *Phaedrus* as a whole, in a devious and often whimsical way, both satirizes rhetoric and its enthusiasts and hints at what could be put in its place, what rhetoric with a proper intellectual and moral foundation might look like. This confrontation of the real and the ideal is typical of Plato.

It would not be surprising if a writer such as Plato, raised in a city at the peak of its literary achievements, familiar with the best that had been produced in the great poetic genres, acquainted with the works of the greatest thinkers of his time, and trained in scepticism by the charismatic Socrates, should have thought long and deeply about the form and nature of his own writings. Tradition had it that he tried again and again to find the best arrangement of words in the first sentence of the *Republic*, writing it out repeatedly in different forms (Dionysius, *On the Composition of Words* 25 and other sources). This intense self-criticism extends to larger spheres. We have already said that the dialogue form allows him to reserve his own position, to end a discussion indecisively, to revisit the same questions in different contexts and through different eyes. The *Phaedrus* more than most works seems to play with the notion of its own inadequacy to complete the enquiry it contains. In several passages the main discussion is dismissed as 'fun' or 'entertainment' (265b, 278b). In the last few pages doubt is cast on the very possibility of a satisfactory formulation of any serious account of a topic in written form, detached from the living activity of oral conversation. But it would be a mistake for the reader to conclude that Plato has ironically denied any significance to his own work; what matters is to recognize that the dialogues do not offer a complete doctrine or a solution to the issues raised. Nevertheless, to raise those issues and to present them in such delightfully thought-provoking form is itself a positive achievement. The words Alcibiades uses about Socrates' conversations can be transferred to his disciple and creator, and applied to the enigma of the Platonic dialogue itself – outwardly bantering and ironic, inwardly profound:

... his arguments, when you really look at them, are also just like Silenus-figures. If you decided to listen to one, it would strike you at first as ludicrous. On the face of it, it's just a collection of irrelevant words and phrases; but these are just the outer skin of this trouble-making satyr. It's all donkeys and bronzesmiths, shoemakers and tanners. He always seems to be repeating himself, and people who haven't heard him before, and aren't too quick on the uptake, laugh at what he says. But look beneath the surface, and get inside them, and you'll find two things. In the first place, they're the only arguments which really make any sense; on top of that they are supremely inspiring, because they contain countless models of excellence and pointers towards it. In fact, they deal with everything you should be concerned about, if you want to lead a good and noble life.

(*Symp.* 221e–2a)

R. B. Rutherford

I am grateful to Tom Griffith for his encouraging comments, and also my colleague Lindsay Judson and my former pupil Charlie Marshall, who both read and criticized the introduction in draft.

xxvi

SELECT BIBLIOGRAPHY

The Greek text of these dialogues is printed, with a facing translation more literal than the version in this volume, in the useful commentaries on both works by C. J. Rowe (*Phaedrus* 1986; *Symposium* 1998). There is also a short commentary on the *Symposium* by K. J. Dover (Cambridge, 1980).

Most of Plato's works are readily available in English translations, e.g. from the Penguin Classics and the Hackett Library. For a convenient one-volume compilation, which includes all but a few works which are probably spurious, see *Plato: Complete Works*, ed. John M. Cooper (Hackett Publishing Co., 1997). The reader who has enjoyed the *Symposium* and the *Phaedrus* should probably turn next to the *Protagoras* and *Gorgias*, and after that to the much longer *Republic*.

The historical context of Greek society is well described by A. Andrewes, *The Greeks* (Penguin *Greek Society*, 1967) and by J. K. Davies, *Democracy and Classical Greece* (1978, revised edn Fontana, 1993). A short but expert account of Socrates is by C. C. W. Taylor, *Socrates* (Past Master series, Oxford, 1998); for fuller treatment, see W. K. C. Guthrie, *A History of Greek Philosophy* iii (Cambridge, 1969), which covers the sophists and Socrates himself; the later volumes (iv and v) on Plato are less rewarding. See also G. Vlastos, *Socrates, Ironist and Philosopher* (Cambridge, 1991) and, by the same author, *Socratic Studies* (Cambridge, 1994); A. Nehamas, *The Art of Living: Socratic Reflections from Nietzsche to Foucault* (University of California, 1998).

On homosexuality in Greek life, the authoritative account of the literary and artistic evidence is by K. J. Dover, *Greek Homosexuality* (Duckworth, 1978), which has been criticized but remains indispensable. For more recent treatments of various aspects see D. M. Halperin, *One Hundred Years of Homosexuality* (Routledge, 1990), which includes an essay on the speech of Socrates/Diotima in the *Symposium*; J. Davidson, *Courtesans and Fishcakes: The Consuming Passions of Classical Athens* (HarperCollins, 1997), especially chapter 3. On Plato's conception of love, see G. Vlastos, 'The individual as an object of love in Plato', in his *Platonic Studies* (2nd edn, Princeton, 1981) chapter 1; A. W. Price, *Love and Friendship in Plato and Aristotle* (Oxford, 1989), chapters 1 to 3.

On Plato's career, the survey in the opening chapter of Guthrie, op. cit. vol. iv (1974) is lucid and well-documented; for an eighty-page sketch of his thought, see B. Williams, *Plato: The Invention of*

Philosophy (Phoenix, 1998); more fully, see R. Kraut (ed.), *The Cambridge Companion to Plato* (Cambridge, 1992), which contains essays on many topics, of uneven value, and very full bibliographies. On aspects of the dialogue form and other literary questions, see R. B. Rutherford, *The Art of Plato: Ten Essays in Platonic Interpretation* (Duckworth, 1995).

The following books include discussions of one or both of the dialogues translated here: M. Nussbaum, *The Fragility of Goodness* (Cambridge, 1986); C. L. Griswold, *Self-knowledge in Plato's Phaedrus* (Yale, 1986); G. R. F. Ferrari, *Listening to the Cicadas: A Study of Plato's Phaedrus* (Cambridge, 1987); R. B. Rutherford, cited above; A. Wilson Nightingale, *Genres in Dialogue: Plato and the Construct of Philosophy* (Cambridge, 1995).

CHRONOLOGY

―――――

DATE	AUTHOR'S LIFE	LITERARY CONTEXT
525 BC		Birth of Aeschylus.
500 BC		Heraclitus said to have flourished at this time.
496 BC		Birth of Sophocles.
490 BC		Birth of Pericles, Athenian statesman, son of Xanthippus and Agariste.
485 BC		
484 BC		Birth of Euripides. Birth of Herodotus, Greek historian.
480 BC		
479 BC		
478 BC		
472 BC		Aeschylus: *Persae.*
469 BC		Birth of Socrates.
468 BC		Sophocles' first victory in tragedy.
460 BC		Birth of Democritus, Greek philosopher. Birth of Hippocrates, Greek physician – to him is ascribed the Hippocratic oath, the earliest and most impressive statement on medical ethics.
458 BC		Aeschylus: *Oresteia.*
456 BC		Death of Aeschylus.
455 BC		Euripides participates in tragic competition for first time. Birth of Thucydides, Greek historian.
450 BC		
449 BC		
447 BC		
446 BC		
444 BC		Birth of Aristophanes.

HISTORICAL EVENTS

Birth of Pheidias, Greek sculptor.

Persian invasion of Sparta. Battle of Marathon.

Death of Darius, ruler of Persia. He is succeeded by his son, Xerxes.

Xerxes defeated at Salamis.
Battles of Artemisium and Thermopylae.
Persians defeated at Plataea.
Delian League against Persia founded by Greeks under Athenian leadership.
Origin of Athenian Empire.

Birth of Alcibiades.
'Peace of Callias' between Athens and Persia – this marks the end of the
war with Persia.
Work begins on the Parthenon under the supervision of the sculptor
Pheidias.
Thirty Years Peace between Sparta and Athens.

PLATO

DATE	AUTHOR'S LIFE	LITERARY CONTEXT
441 BC		(?) Sophocles: *Antigone*.
438 BC		Euripides: *Alcestis*.
		Death of Pindar (b. 518 BC)
432 BC		
431 BC		Euripides produces *Medea*.
430 BC		Birth of Xenophon.
		Socrates serves as a hoplite in the Greek army at Potidaea.
430–428 BC		
428 BC	Plato (Gk *Platon* = broad-shouldered) born in Athens to Ariston and Perictione who both come from aristocratic families. He has two elder brothers, Glaucon and Adeimantus, and a sister, Potane, the mother of Speusippus. For the next twenty years or so, Plato would have received an education in keeping with a boy of noble birth including the study of the Ancient Greek poets. Throughout his youth, Athens is at war.	Death of Anaxagoras. Euripides: *Hippolytus*.
427 BC		Gorgias of Leontini arrives in Athens as an Ambassador. He is chiefly remembered for bringing rhetoric to Athens.
425 BC		Aristophanes: *The Acharnians*.
424 BC		Aristophanes: *The Knights*. Socrates serves as a hoplite at Delium.
423 BC		Aristophanes: *The Clouds* which satirizes the Sophists, and especially Socrates, portraying him as the proprietor of a 'thinking shop'.
422 BC		Aristophanes: *The Wasps*. Socrates serves as a hoplite at Amphipolis where he wins renown for his valour and powers of endurance.

CHRONOLOGY

PLATO

DATE	AUTHOR'S LIFE	LITERARY CONTEXT
421 BC		Aristophanes: *The Peace.*
415 BC		Agathon's first tragic victory, occasion of the drinking-party commemorated in the *Symposium.*
414 BC		Aristophanes: *The Birds.*
412 BC		Birth of Diogenes (d.323 BC), Greek philosopher.
411 BC		Aristophanes: *Lysistrata.*
410 BC		
409 BC	Given Plato's social status, military service at this time can almost be taken for granted. At this age, Plato would have been old enough to take part in military engagements during the last five years of the Peloponnesian War. But records contradict each other as to whether he does see active service. One states that Plato goes on campaigns to Tanagra, Corinth and Delium, and another that Plato 'never saw a battlefield'.	Sophocles: *Philoctetes.*
c.408 BC	Plato's first meeting with Socrates, after which he becomes the older man's disciple.	Euripides writes *The Bacchae* while staying in Macedonia.
407 BC		
406 BC		Death of Euripides.
405 BC		Aristophanes: *The Frogs.* Includes a hilarious fictional contest between Euripides and Aeschylus to decide who is the greatest tragedian. Aeschylus wins. Death of Sophocles.

CHRONOLOGY

PLATO

DATE	AUTHOR'S LIFE	LITERARY CONTEXT
404 BC		
399 BC	Socrates is put on trial for 'impiety' and 'corrupting the minds of the young'. Plato is present at Socrates' trial. Socrates is found guilty by a narrow majority, but by his attitude after the verdict he so enrages his judges that he is sentenced to death. The execution is delayed for thirty days during the Delian festival, and during this time Socrates refuses to avail himself of plans for his escape. He drinks hemlock (the standard method of execution at this time) in the spring of 399 BC. Deeply shocked by Socrates' death, Plato leaves Athens and travels to Megara.	
395 BC	Plato returns to Athens. It is possible that he serves in the battle of Corinth upon his return.	
389 BC	Plato makes the first of three voyages to Sicily, visiting Dionysius I. Perhaps his portrait of the tyrant in the *Republic* is modelled in part on this man.	
388 BC	It is not known when Plato began his dialogues but it is likely that by this time he had completed a large number, including *Ion, Hippias, Protagoras, Apology, Crito, Laches, Lysis, Euthyphro,* and *Gorgias.*	Aristophanes: *Plutus.*

CHRONOLOGY

Athens is taken and handed over to an oligarchy of thirty. Critias and Charmides, respectively cousin and brother of Plato's mother, Perictione, are members of the oligarchy. Roughly 1500 Athenians are murdered during the brief eight-month rule. Socrates refuses to take part in the purges. The oligarchy is overthrown, the thirty being put to death, and democracy restored which lasts throughout Plato's life.

Alcibiades, after again being forced to leave Athens, is murdered by Spartan emissaries.

War between Athens and Corinth.

PLATO

DATE	AUTHOR'S LIFE	LITERARY CONTEXT
387 BC	Plato probably in Italy at this time, and in contact with the Pythagorean philosophers settled there, notably, Archytas.	
386 BC	Plato returns to Athens and founds his Academy about a mile from the City. The Academy includes a grove of trees, gardens, a gymnasium and other buildings, dedicated by Plato to the Muses – patrons of education. Plato lectures in the gymnasium – the public part of the Academy. Among his audience are Speusippus and Xenocrates.	
386– 367 BC	Between these dates it is likely that Plato wrote *Menexenus, Euthydemus, Meno, Cratylus, Symposium, Phaedo, Republic, Phaedrus, Parmenides* and *Theaetetus.*	
384 BC		Birth of Demosthenes (d.322 BC), reputedly the greatest of the Greek orators.
371 BC		Xenophon is expelled and flees to Corinth.
367 BC	At the request of Dion, Plato returns to Sicily with the death of Dionysius I in the hope of persuading Dionysius II to found a colony ruled according to laws devised by Plato himself. He is unsuccessful and, it is rumoured, barely escapes with his life. Some reports even claim that he was sold into slavery by Dionysius II.	
366 BC	Aristotle arrives in Athens. He becomes a student at Plato's Academy and remains there until Plato's death. So outstanding a pupil is Aristotle that Plato calls him 'the reader' and speaks of him as 'the mind of the school'.	

HISTORICAL EVENTS

End of Corinthian War.

Birth of Aristotle.

PLATO

DATE	AUTHOR'S LIFE	LITERARY CONTEXT
361 BC	Plato returns to Sicily for a third time. He is virtually held prisoner in the court of Dionysius but eventually allowed to return after political pressure is put on Dionysius.	
361–347 BC	Between these dates Plato probably writes *Timaeus*, *Critias*, *Sophistes*, *Philebus* and *Laws*.	
357 BC		
355 BC		Death of Xenophon.
353 BC		
347 BC	Plato dies in his 81st year at a wedding feast. At the time of his death he is engaged on the *Laws*. He is succeeded as head of the Academy by his nephew, Speusippus.	
322 BC		Death of Aristotle.

HISTORICAL EVENTS

Dion returns to Sicily at the head of an army and expels Dionysius II (356 BC) – becoming tyrant himself.

Dion of Syracuse assassinated.

SYMPOSIUM

THE SPEAKERS IN THE DIALOGUE

AGATHON, a writer of tragedies
SOCRATES, a truth-loving eccentric
PHAEDRUS, an idealist
PAUSANIAS, a realist – Agathon's lover
ARISTOPHANES, a writer of comedies
ERYXIMACHUS, a doctor
ALCIBIADES, a politician and playboy

PROLOGUE
APOLLODORUS AND A FRIEND

APOLLODORUS: You couldn't have asked anyone better. I live in Phalerum, and the day before yesterday I was going up to town when a man I know caught sight of me disappearing in the distance. He gave me a shout, calling me (a little facetiously) 'You there! Citizen of Phalerum! Hey, Apollodorus! Wait a moment.'

So I stopped and waited.

'Apollodorus,' he said, 'I've been looking for you for ages. I wanted to ask you about the time when Agathon and Socrates and Alcibiades and the others all met for dinner. I want to know what was said about love. I was told about it by a man who had talked to Phoenix, son of Philippus; he said you knew about it as well. He wasn't much help – couldn't remember anything very definite. Can you give me your version? After all, who better than you to talk about Socrates' conversations? For instance, were you at the dinner-party yourself, or not?'

'You must have been given a pretty garbled account, if you think the party you're asking about took place recently enough for me to have been at it.'

'Oh! I thought you were.'

'Really, Glaucon, how could I have been? It's ages since Agathon last lived in Athens, and less than three years since I became friends with

5

Socrates, and got into the habit of keeping up with
what he says and does every day. Before that my life
was just a random whirl of activity. I thought I was
extremely busy, but in fact I was the most pathetic
creature imaginable, just as you are now, doing anything to avoid philosophical thought.'

'Very funny. When *did* the party happen, then?'

'It was when we were still children, when Agathon won the prize with his first tragedy, the day
after he and the members of the chorus made the
usual winners' thanksgivings.'

'Oh, I see. It *was* a long time ago, then. Who told
you about it? Was it Socrates himself?'

'God, no. I got it from the man who told
Phoenix, a man called Aristodemus, from Cyd-
athenaeum. Small man, never wears shoes. He'd
been at the party; in fact, I think he must have been
one of Socrates' keenest admirers in those days. But
I've also asked Socrates about some of the things he
told me, and his version agreed with Aristodemus'.'

'You must tell me all about it, and walking into
town is an ideal opportunity. You can talk, and I
will listen.'

So we discussed the party as we went along, and
that's why, as I said originally, I'm a good person to
ask about it. And if I've got to tell it to you as
well, I'd better get on with it. In any case, I get
tremendous pleasure out of talking about philosophy myself, or listening to other people talk about
it, quite apart from thinking it's good for me. Other
conversation, especially your kind, about money or
business, bores me stiff. You're my friends, but I
feel sorry for you, because you think you're getting

173

b

c.

somewhere, when you're not. You in turn probably think me misguided, and you may well be right. However, I don't *think* you are misguided; I know for certain you are.

FRIEND: Still the old Apollodorus we know and love. Never a good word for yourself or anyone else. As far as I can see, you regard absolutely everyone, starting with yourself, as a lost cause – except for Socrates, that is. I don't know where you picked up the nickname 'softy'; it certainly doesn't fit your conversation – always full of fury against yourself, and everyone else apart from Socrates.

APOLLODORUS: And if that's my opinion of myself and the rest of you, then obviously I'm crazy, or mistaken, I suppose.

FRIEND: Let's not argue about that now, Apollodorus. Just do as I ask, and tell me what was said at Agathon's party.

APOLLODORUS: The conversation went something like this ... or better, let me try to tell it to you right from the beginning, as Aristodemus told it to me.

ARISTODEMUS' ACCOUNT

I met Socrates, all washed and brushed, and wearing shoes (a thing he hardly ever did). I asked him where he was going looking so elegant.

'I'm going to dinner with Agathon. I avoided the first celebration last night; I couldn't face the crowd. But I said I'd come this evening. I'm looking elegant, because Agathon always looks elegant. What about you? How do you feel about coming to dinner uninvited?'

b

'I'll do anything you tell me.'

'Come on then. Let's ignore the proverb, "good men come uninvited to lesser men's feasts", or rather let's change it, to "good men come uninvited to Agathon's feast". After all, Homer does worse than ignore it; he completely contradicts it. His Agamemnon is an outstanding warrior, while his Menelaus is a man of straw. But when Agamemnon is sacrificing and feasting Homer lets Menelaus come to the feast without an invitation, though that's a case of a lesser man coming to dinner with a better.'

c

'I'm afraid, in my case, that Homer is likely to be nearer the mark than you, Socrates. It'll be a question of a nonentity coming to dinner uninvited with a wise man. You'd better decide what you'll say if you do take me. I'm not coming uninvited – only as your guest.'

d

'Two heads are better than one. We'll think of something to say. Come on.'

So off we went. But Socrates, absorbed in his own thoughts, got left behind on the way. I was going to wait for him, but he told me to go on ahead. So I turned up at Agathon's house by myself, and found the door open. In fact, it was slightly embarrassing, because one of the house-slaves met me, and took me straight in, where I found the others had just sat down to dinner. Agathon saw me come in, and at once said, 'Aristodemus, you're just in time to have dinner with us. I hope that's what you've come for. If not, it'll have to wait for another time. I tried to get hold of you yesterday, to ask you, but couldn't find you. But why haven't you got Socrates with you?'

I turned round and looked behind me, and couldn't see Socrates anywhere. So I explained that I had come with Socrates. In fact, but for his invitation, I wouldn't have come at all.

'I'm glad you did. But where is he?'

'He was right behind me just now. I've no more idea than you where he could have got to.'

Agathon turned to a slave. 'Could you go and look for Socrates, please, and ask him in? Aristodemus, why don't you sit over there by Eryximachus?'

While one slave was giving me a wash, so I could sit down to dinner, another slave came in: 'That Socrates you asked me to look for has gone wandering up to the front door of the wrong house. He's just standing there. I asked him to come in but he won't.'

'How odd. Still, don't give up. Keep on asking him.'

But I said, 'No, leave him alone. He's always doing this. It doesn't matter where he is. He just b wanders off and stands there. I don't think he'll be long. Don't badger him; just leave him.'

'Well, if you say so, I suppose we'd better.' He turned to the slaves. 'The rest of us will eat now. Serve the meal just as you like. No one's going to tell you how to do it, any more than I ever tell you. Imagine we're all your guests, and try to give us a c meal we'll enjoy.'

So we started having dinner, though still no sign of Socrates. Agathon kept wanting to send people to look for him, but I wouldn't let him. When he did turn up, he hadn't been long by his standards, but even so we were about halfway through dinner. Agathon, who'd sat down last, at a table on his own, said, 'Come and sit next to me, Socrates. Then d perhaps I shall absorb whatever it was you were thinking about outside. You must have found the answer, or you wouldn't have come in to join us.'

Socrates sat down. 'Wouldn't it be marvellous, Agathon,' he said, 'if ideas were the kind of things which could be imparted simply by contact, and those of us who had few could absorb them from those who had a lot in the same sort of way that liquid can flow from a full container to an empty one if you put a piece of string between them? If that's the nature of ideas, then I think I'm lucky to e be sitting next to you, and getting a nice, substantial transfusion. My ideas aren't much use. They have an ambiguous, dreamlike quality, whereas yours are brilliant, and with so much scope for further improvement. You're only young, and yet they were particularly brilliant the day before yesterday, as more than thirty thousand Greeks can testify.'

'You're a troublemaker, Socrates. But we can settle this question of ideas a bit later. We'll give Dionysus the casting vote, but you'd better have dinner first.'

176   So Socrates sat down and ate, with the others. We poured offerings, sang hymns, and did all the usual things. Then our thoughts turned to drinking, and Pausanias made a suggestion. 'Well, gentlemen, how can we make things as painless for ourselves as possible? I must admit to feeling rather frail after yesterday evening. I need a breather, and I expect most of you do, too. After all, you were there as
b   well. So, how can we make our drinking as painless as possible?'

ARISTOPHANES: I couldn't agree more, Pausanias. Whatever else we do, we don't want to let ourselves in for another evening's hard drinking. I'm one of those who sank without trace last night.

ERYXIMACHUS: I'm glad you both feel like that. But we ought also to consider how strong Agathon is feeling.

AGATHON: Not at all strong.

ERYXIMACHUS: It would certainly be a stroke
c   of luck for people like Aristodemus and Phaedrus and me, if you hard drinkers are prepared to take an evening off. We're not in your league. I'm not worried about Socrates — he's equally happy either way, so he won't mind what we do. But as far as I can see, no one here is all that keen on drinking a

lot, so perhaps I can tell you the truth about getting drunk without causing too much offence. My experience as a doctor leaves me in no doubt that getting drunk is bad for you. I'm not keen on   d drinking to excess myself, and I wouldn't advise anyone else to, especially anyone who still had a hangover from yesterday.

PHAEDRUS: Well, I generally follow your advice, especially on medical matters. So will the others, if they have any sense.

So we all agreed just to drink what we felt like,   c rather than treating it as an opportunity to get drunk.

ERYXIMACHUS: Good, that's settled then. We'll all drink as much as we feel like, and there's no compulsion on anyone. And since we've got that sorted out, I've another suggestion to make. I don't think we need this flute girl who's just started playing. She can play to herself, or to the women upstairs, if she feels like it, but for this evening I suggest *we* stick to conversation. And I've an idea what we might talk about, if you want to hear it.   177

Everyone said they did want to hear it, and urged him to make his suggestion.

ERYXIMACHUS: I'll begin with the words of Euripides' *Melanippe*: 'not mine the tale' I have to tell. Rather it belongs to Phaedrus here. He gets quite worked up about it. 'Don't you think it's odd, Eryximachus,' he says, 'that most of the other gods have had hymns and songs of praise written to them by the poets, but never a word in praise of Eros, the oldest and greatest god? And it's not for want of   b good poets, either. Or think of the great teachers –

they've recorded the exploits of Heracles and other heroes, in prose. Prodicus, for example, does that sort of thing beautifully. Now maybe that's not very surprising, but I came across a book the other day, by a well-known writer, with an extraordinary eulogy in it on the value of salt. You can find any number of things singled out for praise in this way. What is surprising is that there should be so much enthusiasm for that kind of thing, and yet no one, up to the present day, has ever found himself able to praise Eros as he deserves. He is a remarkable god, but he has been totally neglected.'

I agree with Phaedrus. I'd like to do him a favour and make my contribution. What's more, the present gathering seems an ideal opportunity to praise the god. So, if you agree, we can quite happily spend our time in talk. I propose that each of us in turn, going round anti-clockwise, should make a speech, the best he can, in praise of Eros. Phaedrus can start, since he is in the position of honour, and since the whole thing was his idea.

SOCRATES: I don't think anyone will vote against you, Eryximachus. I'm certainly not going to refuse, since love is the only thing I ever claim to know anything about. Agathon and Pausanias won't mind – still less Aristophanes, whose whole life revolves around Dionysus and Aphrodite. In fact I can't see anyone here who *will* object. It's a little unfair on those of us sitting here in the last positions. Still, if you first speakers speak well enough, we shan't have to worry. Good luck, Phaedrus. You go first, and make your speech in praise of Eros.

They all agreed with Socrates, and told Phaedrus

to start. Aristodemus couldn't remember the exact 178
details of everybody's speech, nor in turn can I
remember precisely what he said. But I can give you
the gist of those speeches and speakers which were
most worth remembering.

Phaedrus, as I said, began – something like this.

PHAEDRUS

Eros is a great god, a marvel to men and gods alike.
This is true in many ways, and it is especially true
of his birth. He is entitled to our respect, as the
oldest of the gods – as I can prove. Eros has no   b
parents, either in reality or in works of prose and
poetry. Take Hesiod, for example. All he says is
that in the beginning there was Chaos. '. . . and then
came the full-breasted Earth, the eternal and
immovable foundation of everything, and Eros'.
Acusilaus agrees with Hesiod, that after Chaos
there were just these two, Earth and Eros. And
then there's Parmenides' theory about his birth, that
'Eros was created first of the Gods'. So there is
widespread agreement that Eros is of great   c
antiquity. And being very old he also brings us very
great benefits. I can see nothing better in life for a
young boy, as soon as he is old enough, than finding
a good lover, nor for a lover than finding a boyfriend. Love, more than anything (more than family,
or position, or wealth), implants in men the thing
which must be their guide if they are to live a good
life. And what is that? It is a horror of what is   d
degrading, and a passionate desire for what is
good. These qualities are essential if a state or an

individual is to accomplish anything great or good.
Imagine a man in love being found out doing something humiliating, or letting someone else do
something degrading to him, because he was too
cowardly to stop it. It would embarrass him more
to be found out by the boy he loved than by his
father or his friends, or anyone. And you can see
just the same thing happening with the boy. He is
more worried about being caught behaving badly
by his admirers than by anyone else. So if there were
some way of arranging that a state, or an army,
could be made up entirely of pairs of lovers, it is
impossible to imagine a finer population. They
would avoid all dishonour, and compete with one
another for glory: in battle, this kind of army,
though small, fighting side by side could conquer
virtually the whole world. After all, a lover would
sooner be seen by anyone deserting his post or
throwing away his weapons, rather than by his boyfriend. He would normally choose to die many
times over instead. And as for abandoning the boy,
or not trying to save him if he is in danger – no one
is such a coward as not to be inspired with courage
by Eros, making him the equal of the naturally brave
man. Homer says, and rightly, that god breathes fire
into some of his heroes. And it is just this quality,
whose origin is to be found within himself, that
Eros imparts to lovers.

What is more, lovers are the only people prepared
to die for others. Not just men, either; women also
sometimes. A good example is Alcestis, the daughter of Pelias. She alone was willing to die for her
husband. He had a father and mother, but she so

e

179

b

c

far surpassed them in devotion, because of her passion for him, that she showed them to be strangers to their son, relations in name only. In so doing she was thought, by men and gods alike, to have performed a deed of supreme excellence. Indeed the gods were so pleased with her action that they brought her soul back from the underworld – a privilege they granted to only a fortunate handful of the many people who have done good deeds. That shows how highly even the gods value loyalty and courage in love. Orpheus the son of Oeagrus, on the other hand, was sent away from the underworld empty-handed; he was shown a mere phantom of the woman he came to find, and not given the woman herself. Of course Orpheus was a musician, and the gods thought he was a bit of a coward, lacking the courage to die for his love, as Alcestis did, but trying to find a way of getting into the underworld alive. They punished him further for that, giving him death at the hands of women.

d

In contrast, the man whom the gods honoured above all was Achilles, the son of Thetis. They sent him to the Islands of the Blessed. His mother had warned him that if he killed Hector he would himself be killed, but if he didn't, he would return home and live to a ripe old age. Nevertheless out of loyalty to his lover Patroclus he chose without hesitation to die – not to save him, but to avenge him; for Patroclus had already been killed. The gods were full of admiration, and gave him the highest possible honour, because he valued his lover so highly.

e

180

Incidentally, Aeschylus' view, that it was Achilles who was in love with Patroclus, is nonsense. Quite apart from the fact that he was more beautiful than Patroclus (and than all the other Greek heroes, come to that) and had not yet grown a beard, he was also, according to Homer, much younger. And he must have been younger, because it is an undoubted fact that the gods, though they always value courage which comes from love, are most impressed and pleased, and grant the greatest rewards, when the younger man is loyal to his lover, than when the lover is loyal to him. That's because the lover is a more divine creature than the younger man, since he is divinely inspired. And that's why they honoured Achilles more than Alcestis, and sent him to the Islands of the Blessed.

b

There you are then. I claim that Eros is the oldest of the gods, the most deserving of our respect, and the most useful, for those men, past and present, who want to attain excellence and happiness.

c

That was the gist of Phaedrus' speech. After him, several other people spoke, but Aristodemus couldn't really remember what they said. So he left them out and recounted Pausanias' speech.

PAUSANIAS

Phaedrus, I don't think we've been very accurate in defining our subject for discussion. We've simply said that we must make a speech in praise of Eros. That would be fine, if there were just one Eros. In fact, however, there isn't. And since there isn't, we would do better to define first which Eros we are to praise. I am going to try to put things straight – first defining which Eros we are supposed to be

d

praising, and then trying to praise the god as he deserves.

We are all well aware, I take it, that without Eros there is no Aphrodite. If there were only one Aphrodite, there would be one Eros. However, since there are in fact two Aphrodites, it follows that Eros likewise must be two. There's no doubt about there being two Aphrodites; the older has no mother, and is the daughter of Heaven. We call her Heavenly Aphrodite. The younger is the daughter of Zeus and Dione, and we call her Common Aphrodite. It follows that the Eros who assists this Aphrodite should also, properly speaking, be called Common Eros, and the other Heavenly Eros. We certainly ought to praise all the gods, but we should also attempt to define what is the proper province of each.

It is in general true of any activity that, simply in itself, it is neither good nor bad. Take what we're doing now, for example – that is to say drinking, or singing, or talking. None of these is good or bad in itself, but each becomes so, depending on the way it is done. Well and rightly done, it is good; wrongly done, it is bad. And it's just the same with loving, and Eros. It's not all good, and doesn't all deserve praise. The Eros we should praise is the one which encourages people to love in the right way.

The Eros associated with Common Aphrodite is, in all senses of the word, common, and quite haphazard in his operation. This is the love of the man in the street. For a start, he is as likely to fall in love with women as with boys. Secondly, he falls in love with their bodies rather than their minds.

Thirdly, he picks the most unintelligent people he can find, since all he's interested in is the sexual act. He doesn't care whether it's done in the right way or not. That is why the effect of this Eros is haphazard – sometimes good, sometimes the reverse. This love derives its existence from the much younger Aphrodite, the one composed equally of the female and male elements.

c

The other Eros springs from Heavenly Aphrodite, and in the first place is composed solely of the male element, with none of the female (so it is the love of boys we are talking about), and in the second place is older, and hence free from lust. In consequence, those inspired by this love turn to the male, attracted by what is naturally stronger and of superior intelligence. And even among those who love boys you can tell the ones whose love is purely heavenly. They fall in love only with boys old enough to think for themselves – in other words, with boys who are nearly grown up.

d

Those who start a love affair with boys of that age are prepared, I think, to be friends, and live together, for life. The others are deceivers, who take advantage of youthful folly, and then quite cheerfully abandon their victims in search of others. There ought really to be a law against loving young boys, to stop so much energy being expended on an uncertain end. After all, no one knows how good or bad, in mind and body, young boys will eventually turn out. Good men voluntarily observe this rule, but the common lovers I am talking about should be compelled to do the same, just as we stop them, so far as we can, falling in love with free

e

women. They are actually the people who have 182
brought the thing into disrepute, with the result that
some people even go so far as to say that it is wrong
to satisfy your lover. It is the common lover they
have in mind when they say this, regarding his
demands as premature and unfair to the boy. Surely
nothing done with restraint and decency could
reasonably incur criticism.

What is more, while sexual conventions in other
states are clear-cut and easy to understand, here and
in Sparta, by contrast, they are complex. In Elis, for
example, or Boeotia, and places where they are not b
sophisticated in their use of language, it is laid
down, quite straightforwardly, that it is right to
satisfy your lover. No one, old or young, would say
it was wrong, and the reason, I take it, is that they
don't want to have all the trouble of trying to
persuade them verbally, when they're such poor
speakers. On the other hand, in Ionia and many
other places under Persian rule, it is regarded as
wrong. That is because the Persians' system of government (tyrannies) makes them distrust it, just as
they distrust philosophy and communal exercise. It
doesn't suit the rulers that their subjects should c
think noble thoughts, nor that they should form
the strong friendships or attachments which these
activities and in particular love tend to produce.
Tyrants here in Athens learned the same lesson, by
experience. The relationship between Harmodius
and his lover, Aristogeiton, was strong enough to
put an end to the tyrants' rule.

In short, the convention that satisfying your
lover is wrong is a result of the moral weakness

of those who observe the convention – the rulers'
desire for power, and their subjects' cowardice. The

d   belief that it is always right can be attributed to
mental laziness. Our customs are much better but,
as I said, not easy to understand. Think about it –
let's take the lover first. Open love is regarded better
than secret love, and so is love of the noblest and
best people, even if they are not the best-looking.
In fact, there is remarkable encouragement of the
lover from all sides. He is not regarded as doing

e   anything wrong; it is a good thing if he gets what
he wants, and a shame if he doesn't. And when it
comes to trying to get what he wants, we give the
lover permission to do the most extraordinary
things and be applauded for them – things which if

183   he did them with any other aim or intention, would
cover him in reproach. Think of the way lovers
behave towards the boys they love – think of the
begging and entreating involved in their demands,
the oaths they swear, the nights they spend sleeping
outside the boys' front doors, the slavery they are
prepared to endure (which no slave would put up
with). If they behaved like this for money, or position, or influence of any kind, they would be told
to stop by friends and enemies alike. Their enemies

b   would call their behaviour dependent and servile,
while their friends would censure them sharply, and
even be embarrassed for them. And yet a lover can
do all these things, and be approved of. Custom
attaches no blame to his actions, since he is
reckoned to be acting in a wholly honourable way.
The strangest thing of all is that, in most people's
opinion, the lover has a unique dispensation from

the gods to swear an oath and then break it. Lovers'
vows, apparently, are not binding.

So far, then, gods and men alike give all kinds of
licence to the lover, and an observer of Athenian   c
life might conclude that it was an excellent thing,
in this city, both to be a lover and to be friendly to
lovers. But when we come to the boy, the position
is quite different. Fathers give their sons escorts,
when men fall in love with them, and don't allow
them to talk to their lovers – and those are the
escort's instructions as well. The boy's peers and
friends jeer at him if they see anything of the kind
going on, and when their elders see them jeering,   d
they don't stop them, or tell them off, as they should
if the jeers were unjustified. Looking at this side of
things, you would come to the opposite conclusion
– that this kind of thing is here regarded as highly
reprehensible.

The true position, I think, is this. Going back to
my original statement, there isn't one single form
of love. So love is neither right nor wrong in itself.
Done rightly, it is right; done wrongly, it is wrong.
It is wrong if you satisfy the wrong person, for the
wrong reasons, and right if you satisfy the right
person, for the right reasons. The wrong person is
the common lover I was talking about – the one   e
who loves the body rather than the mind. His love
is not lasting, since *what* he loves is not lasting
either. As soon as the youthful bloom of the body
(which is what he loves) starts to fade, he 'spreads
his wings and is off', as they say, making a mockery
of all his speeches and promises. On the other hand,
the man who loves a boy for his good character will

stick to him for life, since he has attached himself to what is lasting.

184   Our customs are intended to test these lovers well and truly, and get the boys to satisfy the good ones, and avoid the bad. That's why we encourage lovers to chase after boys, but tell the boys not to be caught. In this way we set up a trial and a test, to see which category the lover comes in, and which category the boy he loves comes in. This explains a number of things — for instance, why it's thought wrong for a boy to let himself be caught too quickly. It is felt that some time should elapse, since time is a good test of most things. Also why it is wrong to

b   be caught by means of money or political influence — whether it's a case of the boy being threatened, and yielding rather than holding out, or a case of being offered some financial or political inducement, and not turning it down. No affair of this kind is likely to be stable or secure, quite apart from the fact that it is no basis for true friendship.

There is just one way our customs leave it open for a boy to satisfy his lover and not be blamed for it. It is permissible, as I have said, for a lover to

c   enter upon any kind of voluntary slavery he may choose, and be the slave of the boy he loves. This is not regarded as self-seeking, or in any way demeaning. Similarly there is one other kind of voluntary slavery which is not regarded as demeaning. This is the slavery of the boy, in his desire for improvement. It can happen that a boy chooses to serve a man, because he thinks that by association with him he will improve in wisdom in some way, or in some other form of goodness. This kind of voluntary slavery, like the other, is widely held among us not to be wrong, and not to be self-seeking.

So it can only be regarded as right for a boy to satisfy his lover if both these conditions are satisfied – both the lover's behaviour and the boy's desire for wisdom and goodness. Then the lover and the boy have the same aim, and each has the approval of convention – the lover because he is justified in performing any service he chooses for a boy who satisfies him, the boy because he is justified in submitting, in any way he will, to the man who can make him wise and good. So if the lover has something to offer in the way of sound judgement and moral goodness, and if the boy is eager to accept this contribution to his education and growing wisdom, then, and only then, this favourable combination makes it right for a boy to satisfy his lover. In no other situation is it right.

Nor, in this situation, is there any disgrace in making a mistake, whereas in all other situations it is equally a disgrace to be mistaken or not. For example, suppose a boy satisfies his lover for money, taking him to be rich. If he gets it wrong, and doesn't get any money, because the lover turns out to be poor, it is still regarded as immoral, because the boy who does this seems to be revealing his true character, and declaring that he would do anything for anyone in return for money. And that is not a good way to behave. Equally, a boy may satisfy a man because he thinks he is a good man, and that he himself will become better through his friendship. If he gets it wrong, and his lover turns

d

e

185

b   out to be a bad man, of little moral worth, still there is something creditable about his mistake. He too seems to have revealed his true character – namely, that he is eager to do anything for anyone in return for goodness and self-improvement. And this is the finest of all qualities.

So it is absolutely correct for boys to satisfy their lovers, if it is done in pursuit of goodness. This is the love which comes from the heavenly goddess; it is itself heavenly, and of great value to state and individual alike, since it compels both lover and

c   boy to devote a lot of attention to their own moral improvement. All other sorts of love derive from the other goddess, the common one.

Well, Phaedrus, that's the best I can offer, without preparation, on the subject of Eros.

Pausanias paused (sorry about the pun – sophistic influence). After that it was Aristophanes' turn to speak. But he had just got hiccups. I don't know if it was from eating too much, or for some other reason; anyway he was unable to make his speech.

d   All he could say, since Eryximachus, the doctor, happened to be sitting just below him, was this: 'Eryximachus, you're just the man. Either get rid of my hiccups, or speak instead of me until they stop.'

'I'll do both. I'll take your turn to speak, and when you get rid of your hiccups, you can take mine. While I'm speaking, try holding your breath for a long time, to see if they stop. Failing that, gargle

e   with some water. And if they are very severe, tickle your nose and make yourself sneeze. Do that once or twice, and they'll stop, however severe.'

'Will you please speak first, then?' said Aristophanes. 'And I'll do as you suggest.'

ERYXIMACHUS

Pausanias made an impressive start to his speech, but I do not think he brought it to a very satisfactory conclusion. So I think it is important that I should try to complete his account. His analysis of the twofold nature of Eros seems to me to be a valuable distinction. But I cannot accept his implication that Eros is found only in human hearts, and is aroused only by human beauty. I am a doctor by profession, and it has been my observation, I would say, throughout my professional career, that Eros is aroused by many other things as well, and that he is found also in nature — in the physical life of all animals, in plants that grow in the ground, and in virtually all living organisms. My conclusion is that he is great and awe-inspiring, this god, and that his influence is unbounded, both in the human realm and in the divine.

I will begin by talking about my medical experience, to show my respect for my profession. The nature of the human body shows this twofold Eros, since it is generally agreed that health and sickness in the body are separate and unalike, and that unlike is attracted to unlike, and desires it. So there is one force of attraction for the healthy, and another for the sick. Pausanias was talking just now about it being right to satisfy men, if they are good men, but wrong if all they are interested in is physical pleasure. It is just the same with the body. It is

186

b

c

right to satisfy the good and healthy elements in the body, and one should do so. We call this 'medicine'. Conversely it is wrong to satisfy the bad, unhealthy elements, and anyone who is going to be a skilled doctor should deny these elements.

Medical knowledge is thus essentially knowledge of physical impulses or desires for ingestion or evacuation. In this, the man who can distinguish healthy desires from unhealthy is the best doctor. Moreover he needs the ability to change people's desires, so that they lose one and gain another. There are people who lack desires which they should have. If the doctor can produce these desires, and remove the existing ones, then he is a good doctor. He must, in fact, be able to reconcile and harmonize the most disparate elements in the body. By 'the most disparate' I mean those most opposed to one another – cold and hot, bitter and sweet, dry and wet, and so forth. It was by knowing how to produce mutual desire and harmony among these that our forerunner Asclepius, as the poets say (and I believe) established this art of ours.

Medicine, then, as I say, is completely governed by this god. Likewise physical training, and farming. Music too is no exception, as must be clear to anyone who gives the matter a moment's thought. Perhaps that is what Heraclitus means, though he does not actually express it very clearly, when he says that 'the One' is 'in conflict and harmony with itself', 'like the stringing of a bow or lyre'. Clearly there is a contradiction in saying that a harmony is in conflict, or is composed of conflicting elements. Perhaps what he meant was that, starting from initially discordant high and low notes, the harmony is created only when these are brought into agreement by the skill of the musician. Clearly there could be no harmony between high and low, if they were still in conflict. For harmony is a consonance, and consonance is a kind of agreement. Thus it is impossible that there should be a harmony of conflicting elements, in which those elements still conflict, nor can one harmonize what is different, and incapable of agreement. Or take rhythm as another example; it arises out of the conflict of quick and slow, but only when they cease to conflict. Here it is the art of music which imposes harmony on all the elements, by producing mutual attraction and agreement between them, whereas in the body it is the art of medicine. So music, again, is knowledge of Eros applied to harmony and rhythm.

In the actual formation of harmony and rhythm it is a simple matter to detect the hand of Eros, which at this stage is not the twofold Eros. It is altogether more complicated when we come to apply rhythm and harmony to human activity, either to the making of music, which we call composing, or to the correct use of melody and tempo in what we call education. This really does demand a high degree of skill. And the same argument again holds good, that one should satisfy the most well-ordered people, in the interests of those as yet less well-ordered; one should pay due regard to their desires, which are in fact the good, heavenly Eros, companion of the heavenly muse, Ourania. Common Eros, by contrast, goes with the common muse, Polymnia. The greatest caution is called for

c

d

e

in its employment, if one is to gain enjoyment from it without encouraging pure self-indulgence. Similarly, in my profession, there is a great art in the correct treatment of people's desire for rich food, so that they can enjoy it without ill effects.

Thus in music and medicine, and in all other spheres of activity, human and divine, we must keep a careful eye, so far as is practicable, on both forms of Eros. For both are present. The seasons of the year likewise fully illustrate their joint operation. When all the things I was talking about just now (such as hot and cold, wet and dry) hit upon the right Eros in their relation to one another, and consequently form the right sort of mixture and harmony, then they bring what is seasonable and healthy, both to men and to the rest of the world of animals and plants, and all is as it should be. But when the other Eros, in violence and excess, takes over in the natural seasons of the year, it does all sorts of damage, and upsets the natural order. When that happens the result, generally, is plague and a variety of diseases – for animals and plants alike. Frost, hail and mildew are the result of this kind of competition and disorder involving Eros. Knowledge of Eros in connection with the movements of the stars and the seasons of the year is called astronomy.

Then again, all sacrifices, and everything which comes under the direction of the prophetic arts (that is to say, the whole relationship of gods and men to one another) have as their sole concern the observance and correct treatment of Eros. If, in their behaviour towards their parents, the living and the dead, or the gods, people stop satisfying the good, well-ordered Eros, if they stop honouring him and consulting him in every enterprise, and start to follow the other Eros, then the result is all kinds of wickedness. So the prophetic arts have to keep an eye on, and treat, the two forms of Eros. Their knowledge of Eros in human affairs, the Eros who is conducive to piety and correct observance, makes them the architects of friendship between gods and men.

Such – so great and widespread, in fact universal – is the power possessed, in general by all Eros, but in particular by the Eros which, in the moral sphere, acts with good sense and justice both among us and among the gods. And not only does it possess absolute power; it also brings us complete happiness, enabling us to be companions and friends both of each other and of our superiors, the gods.

Well, I too may have left a lot out in my praise of Eros, but I have not done so deliberately. And if I have left anything out, it is up to you, Aristophanes, to fill the gap. Or if you intend to praise the god in some other way, go ahead and do that, now that you have got rid of your hiccups.

ARISTOPHANES: Yes, they've stopped, but not without resort to the sneezing treatment. I wondered if it was the 'well-ordered' part of my body which demanded all the noise and tickling involved in sneezing. Certainly the hiccups stopped the moment I tried sneezing.

ERYXIMACHUS: Careful, my dear friend. You haven't started yet, and already you're playing the fool. You'll force me to act as censor for your b   speech, if you start fooling around as soon as you get a chance to speak in peace.

ARISTOPHANES [*laughing*]: Fair enough, Eryximachus. Regard my remarks so far as unsaid. But don't be too censorious. I'm worried enough already about what I'm going to say – not that it may arouse laughter (after all, there would be some point in that, and it would be appropriate to my profession), but that it may be laughed out of court.

ERYXIMACHUS: Aristophanes, you're trying to eat your cake and have it. Come on, concentrate.

c   You'll have to justify what you say, but perhaps, if I see fit, I will acquit you.

ARISTOPHANES

Well, Eryximachus, I do intend to make a rather different kind of speech from the kind you and Pausanias made. It's my opinion that mankind is quite unaware of the power of Eros. If they were aware of it, they would build vast temples and altars to him, and make great offerings to him. As it is, though it is of crucial importance that this observance should be paid to him, none of these things is done.

d   Of all the gods, Eros is the most friendly towards men. He is our helper, and cures those evils whose cure brings the greatest happiness to the human race. I'll try to explain his power to you, and then you can go off and spread the word to others.

First of all you need to know about human nature and what has happened to it. Our original nature was not as it is now, but quite different. For one thing there were three sexes, rather than the two (male and female) we have now. The third sex was a combination of these two. Its name has survived, though the phenomenon itself has disappeared. This single combination, comprising both male and female, was, in form and name alike, hermaphrodite. Now it survives only as a term of abuse.

Secondly, each human being formed a complete whole, spherical, with back and ribs forming a circle. They had four hands, four legs, and two faces, identical in every way, on a circular neck. They had a single head for the two faces, which looked in opposite directions; four ears, two sets of genitals, and everything else as you'd expect from the description so far. They walked upright, as we do, in whichever direction they wanted. And when they started to run fast, they were just like people doing cartwheels. They stuck their legs straight out all round, and went bowling along, supported on their eight limbs, and rolling along at high speed.

The reason for having three sexes, and of this kind, was this: the male was originally the offspring of the sun, the female of the earth, and the one which was half-and-half was the offspring of the moon, because the moon likewise is half sun and half-earth. They were circular, both in themselves and in their motion, because of their similarity to their parents. They were remarkable for their strength and vigour, and their ambition led them to make an assault upon the gods. The story which Homer tells of the giants, Ephialtes and Otus, is told of them – that they tried to make a way up to heaven, to attack the gods. Zeus and the other gods wondered what to do about them, and couldn't decide. They couldn't kill them, as they had the giants – striking them with thunderbolts and doing away with the whole race – because the worship and sacrifices they received from men would have been done away with as well. On the other hand, they couldn't go on allowing them to behave so outrageously.

In the end Zeus, after long and painful thought, came up with a suggestion. 'I think I have an idea. Men could go on existing, but behave less disgracefully, if we made them weaker. I'm going to cut each of them in two. This will have two advantages: it will make them weaker, and also more useful to us, because of the increase in their numbers. They will walk upright, on two legs. And if it's clear they still can't behave, and they refuse to lead a quiet life, I'll cut them in half again and they can go hopping along on one leg.'

That was his plan. So he started cutting them in two, like someone slicing vegetables for pickling, or slicing eggs with a wire. And each time he chopped one up, he told Apollo to turn the face and the half-neck round towards the cut side (so that the man could see where he'd been split, and be better behaved in future), and then to heal the rest of the wound. So Apollo twisted the faces round and gathered up the skin all round to what is now called the stomach, like a purse with strings. He made a single outlet, and tied it all up securely in the middle of the stomach; this we now call the navel. He smoothed out most of the wrinkles, and formed the chest, using a tool such as cobblers use for smoothing out wrinkles in a hide stretched over a last. He left a few wrinkles, however, those around the stomach itself and the navel, as a reminder of what happened in those far-off days.

When man's natural form was split in two, each half went round looking for its other half. They put their arms round one another, and embraced each other, in their desire to grow together again. They started dying of hunger, and also from lethargy, because they refused to do anything separately. And whenever one half died, and the other was left, the survivor began to look for another, and twined itself about it, either encountering half of a complete woman (i.e. what we now call a woman) or half a complete man. In this way they kept on dying.

Zeus felt sorry for them, and thought of a second plan. He moved their genitals to the front – up till then they had had them on the outside, and had reproduced, not by copulation, but by discharge on to the ground, like grasshoppers. So, as I say, he moved their genitals to the front, and made them use them for reproduction by insemination, the male in the female. The idea was that if, in embracing, a man chanced upon a woman, they could produce children, and the race would increase. If man chanced upon man, they could get full satisfaction from one another's company, then separate, get on with their work, and resume the business of life.

That is why we have this innate love of one another. It brings us back to our original state, trying to reunite us and restore us to our true human form. Each of us is a mere fragment of a man (like

b

c

d

half a tally-stick); we've been split in two, like
filleted plaice. We're all looking for our 'other half'.
Men who are a fragment of the common sex (the
one called hermaphrodite) are womanizers, and
most adulterers are to be found in this category.
Similarly, women of this type are nymphomaniacs
and adulteresses. On the other hand, women who
are part of an original woman pay very little attention to men. Their interest is in women; lesbians
are found in this class. And those who are part of a
male pursue what is male. As boys, because they are
slices of the male, they are fond of men, and enjoy
going to bed with men and embracing them. These
are the best of the boys and young men, since they
are by nature the most manly. Some people call
them immoral – quite wrongly. It is not immorality,
but boldness, courage and manliness, since they
take pleasure in what is like themselves. This is
proved by the fact that, when they grow up and take
part in public life, it's only this kind who prove
themselves men. When they come to manhood,
they are lovers of boys, and don't naturally show
any interest in marriage or producing children; they
have to be forced into it by convention. They're
quite happy to live with one another, and not get
married.

People like this are clearly inclined to have boyfriends or (as boys) inclined to have lovers, because
they always welcome what is akin. When a lover of
boys (or any sort of lover) meets the real thing (i.e.
his other half), he is completely overwhelmed by
friendship and affection and desire, more or less
refusing to be separated for any time at all. These

are the people who spend their whole lives together, and yet they cannot find words for what they want from one another. No one imagines that it's simply sexual intercourse, or that sex is the reason why one gets such enormous pleasure out of the other's company. No, it's obvious that the soul of each has some other desire, which it cannot express. It can only give hints and clues as to its wishes.

    d

Imagine that Hephaestus came and stood over them, with his smith's tools, as they lay in bed together. Suppose he asked them, 'What is it you want from one another, mortals?' If they couldn't tell him, he might ask again, 'Do you want to be together as much as possible, and not be separated, day or night? If that's what you want, I'm quite prepared to weld you together, and make you grow into one. You can be united, the two of you, and live your whole life together, as one. Even down in Hades, when you die, you can be a single dead person, rather than two. Decide whether that's what you want, and whether that would satisfy you.' We can be sure that no one would refuse this offer. Quite clearly, it would be just what they wanted. They'd simply think they'd been offered exactly what they'd always been after, in sexual intercourse, trying to melt into their lovers, and so be united.

    e

So that's the explanation; it's because our original nature was as I have described, and because we were once complete. And the name of this desire and pursuit of completeness is Eros, or love. Formerly, as I say, we were undivided, but now we've been split up by god for our misdeeds – like the Arcadians by the Spartans. And the danger is that, if we

    193

don't treat the gods with respect, we may be divided
again, and go round looking like figures in a bas-
relief, sliced in half down the line of our noses.
We'd be like torn-off counterfoils. That's why we
should all encourage the utmost piety towards the
b   gods. We're trying to avoid this fate, and achieve
the other. So we take Eros as our guide and leader.
Let no one oppose this aim – and incurring divine
displeasure *is* opposing this aim – since if we are
friends with god, and make our peace with him,
we shall find and meet the boys who are part of
ourselves, which few people these days succeed in
doing.

I hope Eryximachus won't misunderstand me,
and make fun of my speech, and say it's about Pausanias and Agathon. Perhaps they do come in this
c   class, and are both males by nature. All I'm saying
is that in general (and this applies to men and
women) this is where happiness for the human race
lies – in the successful pursuit of love, in finding
the love who is part of our original self, and in
returning to our former state. This is the ideal, but
in an imperfect world we must settle for the nearest
to this we can get, and this is finding a boyfriend
who is mentally congenial. And if we want to praise
d   the god who brings this about, then we should
praise Eros, who in this predicament is our great
benefactor, attracting us to what is part of ourselves, and gives us great hope for the future that
he will reward respect for the gods by returning us
to our original condition, healing us, and making
us blessed and perfectly happy.

There you are then, Eryximachus. There is my

speech about Eros. A bit different from yours, I'm afraid. So please, again, don't laugh at it, and let's hear what all the others have to say – or rather, both e the others, since only Agathon and Socrates are left.

ERYXIMACHUS: All right, I won't laugh. In any case, I thought it was a most enjoyable speech. In fact, if I did not know Socrates and Agathon to be experts on love, I would be very worried that they might have nothing to say, so abundant and varied have been the speeches so far. But knowing them as I do, I have no such anxiety.

SOCRATES: It's fine for you, Eryximachus. 194 You've already made an excellent speech. If you were in my shoes – or rather, perhaps, the shoes I will be in when Agathon has made a good speech as well – then you might well be alarmed, and be in precisely the state that I am in now.

AGATHON: Ah! Trying a little black magic, are you, Socrates? Are you hoping it'll make me nervous if I think the audience is expecting a great speech from me?

SOCRATES: Agathon, I've seen your nerve and courage in going up on the platform with the actors, b to present your plays, before the eyes of that vast audience. You were quite unperturbed by that, so it'd be pretty stupid of me to imagine that you'd be nervous in front of the few people here.

AGATHON: I may be stage-struck, Socrates, but I'm still aware that, to anyone with any sense, a small critical audience is far more daunting than a large uncritical one.

SOCRATES: It would be quite wrong for me, of c all people, to suggest that you are lacking in taste or judgement. I'm well aware that in all your contacts with those you consider discriminating, you value their opinion more highly than that of the public. But don't put us in that category – after all, we were there, we were part of 'the public'. Anyway, let's pursue this: if you came across truly discriminating people (not us), you would perhaps be daunted by them, if you thought you were producing something second-rate. Is that right?

AGATHON: It is.

d SOCRATES: Whereas offering the public something second-rate would not worry you, would it?

PHAEDRUS: Agathon, if you answer Socrates, he won't give a thought to the rest of us, so long as he has someone to talk to, particularly someone good-looking. For myself, I love hearing Socrates talk, but it's my job to supervise the progress of the speeches in praise of Eros, and get a speech out of each of you. When you've both paid your tribute to the god, then the two of you can get on with your discussion.

e AGATHON: Quite right, Phaedrus. There's no reason why I shouldn't make my speech. I shall have plenty of other opportunities to talk to Socrates.

AGATHON

I want first to talk about *how* I should talk, and then talk. All the speakers so far have given me the impression that they were not so much praising the god as congratulating mankind on the good things the god provides. No one has told us what the giver of these benefits is really like, in himself. And yet, in any speech of praise on any subject, the only correct procedure is to work systematically through the subject under discussion, saying what its nature is, and what benefits it gives. That is how we too should by rights be praising Eros, describing first his nature, then his gifts.

I claim, then, that though all the gods are blessed, Eros, if I may say this without offending the other gods, is the most blessed, since he is the most beautiful and the best. The most beautiful? Well, for a start, Phaedrus, he is the youngest of the gods. He b proves this himself by running away at top speed from old age. Yet old age is swift enough, and swifter than most of us would like. It is Eros' nature to hate old age, and steer well clear of it. He lives and exists always with the young. 'Birds of a feather', and all that. So, though there was much in Phaedrus' speech with which I agreed, I didn't agree with his claim that Eros was older than Cronus or Iapetus. I would say he's the youngest of the gods – c eternally young, in fact. The earliest troubles among the gods, which Hesiod and Parmenides write about, were, if those writers are correct, the work of Necessity, not of Eros. If Eros had been there, there would have been none of this cutting, or tying, each other up, or any of the other acts of violence. There would have been friendship and peace, as there has been since Eros became king of the gods.

So, he is young. And not only young, but delicate. You need a poet like Homer to show how delicate. d Homer describes Ate as a god and as delicate (or at any rate, with delicate feet): 'delicate are her feet;

she walks not upon the ground, but goes upon the heads of men'. Presumably he's giving an example here to show how delicate – she goes not on what is hard, but on what is soft. We too can use a similar argument to show how delicate Eros is. He does not walk upon the ground, nor yet on men's heads (which aren't that soft anyway); he lives and moves among the softest of all things, making his home in the hearts and minds of gods and men. And not in all hearts equally. He avoids any hard hearts he comes across, and settles among the tender-hearted. He must therefore be extremely delicate, since he only ever touches (either with his feet or in any other way) the softest of the soft.

Very young, then, and very delicate. Another thing about him is that he's very supple. He can't be rigid and unyielding, because he wouldn't be able to insinuate himself anywhere he likes, entering and leaving men's hearts undetected. Eros' outstanding beauty is universally agreed, and this again suggests that he is well-proportioned and supple. Ugliness and Eros are ever at odds with one another. Finally, the beauty of his skin is attested by his love of flowers. He will not settle in a man's body, or heart, or anywhere else, if it is past the first flower and bloom of youth. But he does settle down, and remain, in any flowery and fragrant place.

So much for the god's beauty, though I've left out more than I've said. Now I must say something about his goodness. The main thing about Eros is that no one, god or man, wrongs him or is wronged by him. Nothing is done to him, when it is done, by force. Force cannot touch Eros. When he acts, he

acts without force, since everyone serves Eros quite
willingly, and it's agreed by 'our masters, the laws'
that where there is mutual consent and agreement,
there is justice. Moreover, he is a paragon of virtue
as well as justice. After all, virtue is agreed to be
control of pleasures and desires, and no pleasure is
stronger than love. But if they are weaker than love,
then he has control over them, and if he has control
over pleasures and desires, he must be highly
virtuous.

And what about courage? 'Ares himself cannot
hold his ground' against Eros. Ares does not take
Eros prisoner; it is Eros – the love of Aphrodite, so
the story goes – who takes Ares prisoner, and the
captor is stronger than the captive. He who over-
comes the bravest is himself the bravest of all.

So much for the god's justice, virtue and courage.
Now for his wisdom. I must try as hard as I can not
to leave anything out, and so I too, in my turn, will
start with a tribute to my own profession, following
Eryximachus' example. Eros is an accomplished
poet, so accomplished that he can turn others into
poets. Everyone turns to poetry, 'however philistine
he may have been before', when moved by Eros. We
should take this as an indication that, in general,
Eros is master of all forms of literary or artistic
creation. After all, no one can impart, or teach, a
skill which he does not himself possess or know.
And who will deny that the creation of all living
things is the work of Eros' wisdom, which makes all
living things come into being and grow?

It's the same with any skilled activity. It is common knowledge that those who have this god

for their teacher win fame and reputation; those
he passes by remain in obscurity. For example,
Apollo's discoveries (archery, medicine and prophecy) were all guided by desire and love, so he too
b   can be called a disciple of Eros. Likewise with the
Muses and the arts, Hephaestus and metalworking,
Athene and weaving, and Zeus and 'the governance
of gods and men'. And if we ask why the quarrels
of the gods were settled as soon as Eros appeared,
without doubt the reason was love of beauty (there
being no love of ugliness). In earlier times, as I said
originally, there were many violent quarrels among
the gods – or so we are told – because they were
in the grip of Necessity. But since Eros' birth, all
manner of good has resulted, for gods and men,
from the love of beauty.

c   Such, Phaedrus, is my view of Eros. He stands
out as beautiful and excellent in himself; and secondly, he is the origin of similar qualities in others.
I am tempted to speak in verse, and say he brings

> Sweet peace to men, and calm o'er all the deep,
> Rest to the winds, to those who sorrow, sleep.

d   He gives us the feeling, not of longing, but of
belonging, since he is the moving spirit behind all
those occasions when we meet and gather together.
Festivals, dances, sacrifices – in these he is the moving spirit. Implanter of gentleness, supplanter of
fierceness; generous with his kindness, ungenerous
with unkindness; gracious, gentle; an example to
the wise, a delight to the gods; craved by those
without him, saved by those who have him; of lux-
ury, delicacy, elegance, charm, yearning and desire

he is the father; heedful of the good, heedless of
the bad; in hardship and in fear, in need and in
argument, he is the best possible helmsman, com-   e
rade, ally and saviour; the glory of gods and men;
the best and finest guide, whom every man should
follow, singing glorious praises to him, and sharing
in the song which he sings to enchant the minds of
gods and men.

That is my speech, Phaedrus, in part fun, in part
(as far as I could make it) fairly serious. Let it be an
offering to the god.

When Agathon finished speaking, we all burst   198
into applause. We thought the young man had done
full justice both to himself and to the god.

SOCRATES [*to Eryximachus*]: Well, son of Acumenus, do you still think my earlier fear unfounded?
Wasn't I right when I predicted Agathon would
make a brilliant speech, and there would be nothing
left for me to say?

ERYXIMACHUS: Your prediction was half-true.
Agathon did make a good speech. But I don't think
you will find nothing to say.

SOCRATES: My dear fellow, what is there left for   b
me or anyone else to say, after such a fine and varied
speech? Maybe it wasn't all equally brilliant, but
that bit at the end was enough to silence anyone
with the beauty of its language and phraseology.
When I realized I wasn't going to be able to make
anything like such a good speech, I nearly ran away
and disappeared, in embarrassment, only there was   c
nowhere to go. The speech reminded me of Gorgias, and put me in exactly the position described by
Homer. I was afraid, at the end of his speech there,

that Agathon was going to brandish the head of
Gorgias, the great speaker, at my speech, turning
me to stone and silencing me. I realized then how
fatuous it was to have agreed to take my turn with
you in praising Eros, and to have claimed to be an
expert on love. It turns out now that I know nothing
at all about making speeches of praise. I was naïve
enough to suppose that one should speak the truth
about whatever it was that was being praised, and
that from this raw material one should select the
most telling points, and arrange them as pleasingly
as possible. I was pretty confident I would make
a good speech, because I thought I knew about
speeches of praise. However, it now seems that
praising things well isn't like that; it seems to be a
question of hyperbole and rhetoric, regardless of
truth or falsehood. And if it's false, that's immater-
ial. So our original agreement, as it now seems, was
that each of us should pretend to praise Eros, rather
than really praise him.

That, I imagine, is why you credit Eros with all
the good points you have dug out in his favour. You
say his nature is this, and the blessings he produces
are these; your object is to make him appear as noble
and fine as possible (in the eyes of the ignorant,
presumably, since those who know about Eros
clearly aren't going to believe you). Certainly your
praise of him looks very fine and impressive, but I
didn't realize this was what was called for; if I had
known, I wouldn't have agreed to take my turn in
praising him. 'My tongue promised, not my heart.'
Anyway, it can't be helped, but I don't propose to
go on praising him like that – I wouldn't know how

to. What I am prepared to do, if you like, is tell the
truth, in my own way, and not in competition with   b
your speeches. I don't want to make a complete fool
of myself. What do you think, Phaedrus? Do you
want a speech of that sort? Do you want to hear the
truth told about Eros? And may I use whatever
language and forms of speech come naturally?

Phaedrus and the others told him to make his
speech, in whatever way he thought best.

SOCRATES: One other point before I start,
Phaedrus. Will you let me ask Agathon a few brief
questions? I'd like to get his agreement before I
begin.

PHAEDRUS: Yes, I'll let you. Ask away.   c

So Socrates began his speech, something like
this.

SOCRATES

Well, my dear Agathon, I liked the beginning of
your speech. You said the first thing to do was to
reveal the nature of Eros; after that his achievements. I think that was an excellent starting point.
And since you've explained everything else about
the nature of Eros so impressively and so well, can
you tell me one more thing? Is Eros' nature such   d
that he is love produced by something, or by nothing? I don't mean, is he the son of a father or a
mother — it would be an absurd question, to ask
whether Eros is son of a father or mother. But
suppose I asked you, about this thing 'father',
whether a father is father of something or not? If
you wanted to give an accurate answer, you would

say, presumably, that a father is father of a son or a daughter, wouldn't you?

AGATHON: Yes, I would.

SOCRATES: And the same with a mother?

AGATHON: Yes, the same.

e   SOCRATES: Let's take a few more questions, so you can be quite clear what I mean. Suppose I ask, 'What about a brother, simply as a brother? Is he someone's brother, or not?'

AGATHON: Yes, he is.

SOCRATES: His brother's or sister's, I take it?

AGATHON: Yes.

SOCRATES: Try, then, to answer my question about Eros. Is Eros love of nothing, or of something?

AGATHON: Of something, certainly.

200   SOCRATES: Good. Hold on to that answer. Keep it in mind, and make a mental note what it is that Eros is love of. But first tell me this, this thing which Eros is love of, does he desire it, or not?

AGATHON: Certainly.

SOCRATES: And does he possess that which he desires and loves, or not?

AGATHON: Probably not.

SOCRATES: I'm not interested in probability, but in certainty. Consider this proposition: anything which desires something desires what it does not have, and it only desires when it is lacking something. This proposition, Agathon, seems to me to

b   be absolutely certain. How does it strike you?

AGATHON: Yes, it seems certain to me too.

SOCRATES: Quite right. So would a big man want to be big, or a strong man want to be strong?

AGATHON: No, that's impossible, given what we have agreed so far.

SOCRATES: Because if he possesses these qualities, he cannot also lack them.

AGATHON: True.

SOCRATES: So if a strong man wanted to be strong, or a fast runner to be fast, or a healthy man to be healthy – but perhaps I'd better explain what I'm on about. I'm a bit worried that you may think that people like this, people having these qualities, can also want the qualities which they possess. So I'm trying to remove this misapprehension. If you think about it, Agathon, people cannot avoid possession of whichever of these qualities they do possess, whether they like it or not. So obviously there's no point in desiring to do so. When anyone says, 'I'm in good health, and I also desire to be in good health', or 'I am rich and also desire to be rich', i.e. 'I desire those things which I already have', then we should answer him: 'What you want is to go on possessing, in the future, the wealth, health, or strength you possess now, since you have them now, like it or not. So when you say you desire what you've already got, are you sure you don't just mean you want to continue to possess in the future what you possess now?' Would he deny this?

AGATHON: No, he would agree.

SOCRATES: But isn't this a question of desiring what he doesn't already have in his possession – i.e. the desire that what he does have should be safely and permanently available to him in the future?

AGATHON: Yes, it is.

SOCRATES: So in this, or any other, situation,

the man who desires something desires what is not available to him, and what he doesn't already have in his possession. And what he neither has nor himself is – that which he lacks – this is what he wants and desires.

AGATHON: Absolutely.

SOCRATES: Right then, let's agree on the argument so far. Eros has an existence of his own; he is in the first place love of something, and secondly, he is love of that which he is without.

AGATHON: Yes.

201 SOCRATES: Keeping that in mind, just recall what you said were the objects of Eros, in your speech. I'll remind you, if you like. I think what you said amounted to this: trouble among the gods was ended by their love of beauty, since there could be no love of what is ugly. Isn't that roughly what you said?

AGATHON: Yes, it is.

SOCRATES: And a very reasonable statement too, my friend. And this being so, Eros must have an existence as love of beauty, and not love of ugliness, mustn't he?

AGATHON: Yes.

b SOCRATES: But wasn't it agreed that he loves what he lacks, and does not possess?

AGATHON: Yes, it was.

SOCRATES: So Eros lacks, and does not possess, beauty.

AGATHON: That is the inevitable conclusion.

SOCRATES: Well then, do you describe as beautiful that which lacks beauty and has never acquired beauty?

AGATHON: No.

SOCRATES: If that is so, do you still maintain that Eros is beautiful?

AGATHON: I rather suspect, Socrates, that I didn't know what I was talking about.

SOCRATES: It sounded marvellous, for all that, Agathon. Just one other small point. Would you agree that what is good is also beautiful?   c

AGATHON: Yes, I would.

SOCRATES: So if Eros lacks beauty, and if what is good is beautiful, then Eros would lack what is good also.

AGATHON: I can't argue with you, Socrates. Let's take it that it is as you say.

SOCRATES: What you mean, Agathon, my very good friend, is that you can't argue with the truth. Any fool can argue with Socrates. Anyway, I'll let you off for now, because I want to pass on to you   d
the account of Eros which I once heard given by a woman called Diotima, from Mantinea. She was an expert on this subject, as on many others. In the days before the plague she came to the help of the Athenians in their sacrifices, and managed to gain them a ten-year reprieve from the disease. She also taught me about love.

I'll start from the position on which Agathon and I reached agreement, and I'll give her account, as best I can, in my own words. So first I must explain, as you rightly laid down, Agathon, what Eros is and what he is like; then I must describe   e
what he does. I think it'll be easiest for me to explain things as she explained them when she was questioning me, since I gave her pretty much the same

answers Agathon has just been giving me. I said
Eros was a great god, and a lover of beauty. Diotima
proved to me, using the same argument by which I
have just proved it to Agathon, that, according to
my own argument, Eros was neither beautiful nor
good.

'What do you mean, Diotima,' I said. 'Is Eros
then ugly or bad?'

'Careful what you say. Do you think what is not
beautiful must necessarily be ugly?'

202   'Obviously.'

'And that what is not wise is ignorant? Don't
you realize there is an intermediate state, between
wisdom and ignorance?'

'And what is that?'

'Think of someone who has a correct opinion,
but can give no rational explanation of it. You
wouldn't call this knowledge (how can something
irrational be knowledge?), yet it isn't ignorance
either, since an opinion which accords with reality
cannot be ignorance. So correct opinion is the kind
of thing we are looking for, between understanding
and ignorance.'

'That's true.'

b   'So don't insist that what is not beautiful must
necessarily be ugly, nor that what is not good must
be bad. The same thing is equally true of Eros; just
because, as you yourself admit, he is not good or
beautiful, you need not regard him as ugly and bad,
but as something between these extremes.'

'Yet he is universally agreed to be a great god.'

'By those who don't know what they are talking
about, do you mean? Or those who do?'

'I mean by absolutely everyone.'

Diotima laughed. 'How can Eros be agreed to be a great god by people who don't even admit that   c he's a god at all?'

'What people?'

'Well, you, for one. And me, for another.'

'What do you mean?'

'Quite simple. The gods are all happy and beautiful, aren't they? You wouldn't go so far as to claim that any of the gods is not happy and beautiful?'

'Good Lord, no.'

'And you agree that "happy" means "possessing what is good and beautiful"?'

'Certainly.'

'But you have already admitted that Eros lacks what is good and beautiful, and that he desires them   d because he lacks them.'

'Yes, I have.'

'How can he be a god, then, if he is without beauty and goodness?'

'He can't, apparently.'

'You see, even you don't regard Eros as a god.'

'What can Eros be, then? A mortal?'

'Far from it.'

'What, then?'

'As in the other examples, something between a mortal and an immortal.'

'And what is that, Diotima?'

'A great spirit, Socrates. Spirits are midway between what is divine and what is human.'   e

'What power does such a spirit possess?'

'He acts as an interpreter and means of communication between gods and men. He takes requests and offerings to the gods, and brings back instructions and benefits in return. Occupying this middle position he plays a vital role in holding the world together. He is the medium of all prophecy and religion, whether it concerns sacrifice, forms of worship, incantations, or any kind of divination or sorcery. There is no direct contact between god and man. All association and communication between them, waking or sleeping, takes place through Eros. This kind of knowledge is knowledge of the spirit; any other knowledge (occupational or artistic, for example) is purely utilitarian. Such spirits are many and varied, and Eros is one of them.'

'Who are his parents?'

'That is not quite so simple, but I'll tell you, all the same. When Aphrodite was born, the gods held a banquet, at which one of the guests was Resource, the son of Ingenuity. When they finished eating, Poverty came begging, as you would expect (there being plenty of food), and hung around the doorway. Resource was drunk (on nectar, since wine hadn't been invented), so he went into Zeus' garden, and was overcome by sleep. Poverty, seeing here the solution to her own lack of resources, decided to have a child by him. So she lay with him, and conceived Eros. That's why Eros is a follower and servant of Aphrodite, because he was conceived at her birthday party – and also because he is naturally attracted to what is beautiful, and Aphrodite is beautiful.

'So Eros' attributes are what you would expect of a child of Resource and Poverty. For a start, he's

always poor, and so far from being soft and beautiful (which is most people's view of him), he is hard,
unkempt, barefoot, homeless. He sleeps on the   d
ground, without a bed, lying in doorways or in the
open street. He has his mother's nature, and need
is his constant companion. On the other hand, from
his father he has inherited an eye for beauty and the
good. He is brave, enterprising and determined – a
marvellous huntsman, always intriguing. He is intellectual, resourceful, a lover of wisdom his whole life
through, a subtle magician, sorcerer and thinker.

'His nature is neither that of an immortal nor that   e
of a mortal. In one and the same day he can be
alive and flourishing (when things go well), then
at death's door, later still reviving as his father's
character asserts itself again. But his resources are
always running out, so that Eros is never either
totally destitute or affluent. Similarly he is midway
between wisdom and folly, as I will show you. None
of the gods searches for wisdom, or tries to become
wise – they are wise already. Nor does anyone else   204
wise search for wisdom. On the other hand, the
foolish do not search for wisdom or try to become
wise either, since folly is precisely the failing which
consists in not being fine and good, or intelligent –
and yet being quite satisfied with the way one is.
You cannot desire what you do not realize you lack.'

'Who then are the lovers of wisdom, Diotima, if
they are neither the wise nor the foolish?'

'That should by now be obvious, even to a child.   b
They must be the intermediate class, among them
Eros. We would classify wisdom as very beautiful,
and Eros is love of what is beautiful, so it necessarily

follows that Eros is a lover of wisdom (lovers of wisdom being the intermediate class between the wise and the foolish). The reason for this, too, is to be found in his parentage. His father is wise and resourceful, while his mother is foolish and resourceless.

'Such is the nature of this spirit, Socrates. Your views on Eros revealed a quite common mistake. You thought (or so I infer from your comments) that Eros was what was loved, rather than the lover. That is why you thought Eros was beautiful. After all, what we love really *is* beautiful and delicate, perfect and delightful, whereas the lover has the quite different character I have outlined.'

'Fair enough, my foreign friend, I think you're right. But if that's what Eros is like, what use is he to men?'

'That's the next point I want to explain to you, Socrates. I've told you what Eros is like, and what his parentage is; he is also love of what is beautiful, as you say. Now let's imagine someone asking us, "Why is Eros love of the beautiful, Socrates and Diotima?" Let me put it more clearly: what is it that the lover of beauty desires?'

'To possess it.'

'That prompts the further question, what good does it do someone to possess beauty?'

'I don't quite know how to give a quick answer to that question.'

'Well, try a different question, about goodness rather than beauty: Socrates, what does the lover of goodness want?'

'To possess it.'

'What good will it do him to possess it?'

'That's easier. It will make him happy.'

205

'Yes, because those who are happy are happy because they possess what is good. The enquiry seems to have reached a conclusion, and there is no need to ask the further question, "If someone wants to be happy, why does he want to be happy?"'

'True.'

'Do you think this wish and this desire are common to all mankind, and that everyone wants always to possess what is good? Or what do you think?'

'I think it is common to all men.'

'In that case, Socrates, why do we not describe all men as lovers, if everyone always loves the same thing? Why do we describe some people as lovers, but not others?'

b

'I don't know. I agree with you, it is surprising.'

'Not really. We abstract a part of love, and call it by the name of the whole – love – and then for the other parts we use different names.'

'What names? Give me an example.'

'What about this? Take a concept like creation, or composition. Composition means putting things together, and covers a wide range of activities. Any activity which brings anything at all into existence is an example of creation. Hence the exercise of any skill is composition, and those who practise it are composers.'

c

'True.'

'All the same, they aren't all called composers. They all have different names, and it's only one subdivision of the whole class (that which deals with music and rhythm) which is called by the general

name. Only this kind of creation is called composing, and its practitioners composers.'

'True.'

'Well, it's the same with love. In general, for any-
d   one, any desire for goodness and happiness is love
– and it is a powerful and unpredictable force. But
there are various ways of pursuing this desire –
through money-making, through physical fitness,
through philosophy – which do not entitle their
devotees to call themselves lovers, or describe
their activity as loving. Those who pursue one particular mode of loving, and make that their concern,
have taken over the name of the whole (love, loving
and lovers).'

'You may well be right.'

'There is a theory that lovers are people in
e   search of their other half. But according to my
theory, love is not love of a half, nor of a whole,
unless it is good. After all, men are prepared to
have their own feet and hands cut off, if they think
there's something wrong with them. They're not
particularly attached to what is their own, except
in so far as they regard the good as their own
property, and evil as alien to them. And that's
206   because the good is the only object of human love,
as I think you will agree.'

'Yes, I certainly do agree.'

'Can we say, then, quite simply, that men love
the good?'

'Yes.'

'And presumably we should add that they want
to possess the good?'

'Yes, we should.'

'And not merely to possess it, but to possess it for ever.'

'That also.'

'In short, then, love is the desire for permanent possession of the good.'

'Precisely.'

'If this is always the object of our desire, what is the particular manner of pursuit, and the particular sphere of activity, in which enthusiasm and effort qualify for the title "love"? What is this activity? Do you know?'

'No, I don't. That's why I find your knowledge so impressive. In fact, I've kept coming to see you because I want an answer to just that question.'

'Very well, I'll tell you. The activity we're talking about is the use of what is beautiful for the purpose of reproduction, whether physical or mental.'

'I'm no good at riddles. I don't understand what you mean.'

'I'll try to make myself clearer. Reproduction, Socrates, both physical and mental, is a universal human activity. At a certain age our nature desires to give birth. To do so, it cannot employ an ugly medium, but insists on what is beautiful. Sexual intercourse between man and woman is this reproduction. So there is the divine element, this germ of immortality, in mortal creatures – i.e. conception and begetting. These cannot take place in an uncongenial medium, and ugliness is uncongenial to everything divine, while beauty is congenial. Therefore procreation has beauty as its midwife and its destiny, which is why the urge to reproduce becomes gentle and happy when it comes near beauty: then conception and begetting become possible. By contrast, when it comes near ugliness it becomes sullen and offended, it contracts, withdraws, and shrinks away and does not beget. It stifles the reproductive urge, and is frustrated. So in anyone who is keen (one might almost say bursting) to reproduce, beauty arouses violent emotion, because beauty can release its possessor from the agony of reproduction. Your opinion, Socrates, that love is desire for beauty, is mistaken.'

'What is the correct view, then?'

'It is the desire to use beauty to beget and bear offspring.'

'Perhaps.'

'Certainly! And why to beget? Because begetting is, by human standards, something eternal and undying. So if we were right in describing love as the desire always to possess the good, then the inevitable conclusion is that we desire immortality as well as goodness. On this argument, love must be desire for immortality as much as for beauty.'

Those were her teachings, when she talked to me about love. And one day she asked me, 'What do you think is the reason for this love and this desire? You know how strangely animals behave when they want to mate. Animals and birds, they're just the same. Their health suffers, and they get all worked up, first over sexual intercourse, and then over raising the young. For these ends they will fight, to the death, against far stronger opponents. They will go to any lengths, even starve themselves, to bring up their offspring. We can easily imagine human beings behaving like this from rational motives, but what can be the cause of such altruistic behaviour in animals? Do you know?'   c

'No, I don't.'

'Do you think you can become an expert on love without knowing?'

'Look, Diotima, I know I have a lot to learn. I've just admitted that. That's why I've come to you. So please tell me the cause of these phenomena, and anything else I should know about love.'

'Well, if you believe that the natural object of love is what we have often agreed it to be, then the answer is not surprising, since the same   d reasoning still holds good. What is mortal tries, to the best of its ability, to be everlasting and immortal. It does this in the only way it can, by always leaving a successor to replace what decays. Think of what we call the life-span and identity of an individual creature. For example, a man is said to be the same individual from childhood until old age. The cells in his body are always changing, yet he is still called the same person, despite being perpetually reconstituted as parts of him decay – hair, flesh, bones, blood, his whole body, in fact.   e And not just his body, either. Precisely the same happens with mental attributes. Habits, dispositions, beliefs, opinions, desires, pleasures, pains and fears are all varying all the time for everyone. Some disappear, others take their place. And when we come to knowledge, the situation is even odder.   208 It's not just a question of one piece of knowledge disappearing and being replaced by another, so that we are never the same people, as far as knowledge goes: the same thing happens with each individual piece of knowledge. What we call studying presupposes that knowledge is transient. Forgetting is loss of knowledge, and studying preserves knowledge by creating memory afresh in us, to replace what is lost. Hence we have the illusion of continuing knowledge.

'All continuous mortal existence is of this kind. It is not the case that creatures remain always, in every detail, precisely the same – only the divine does that. It is rather that what is lost, and what decays, always leaves behind a fresh copy of itself. This, Socrates, is the mechanism by which mortal creatures can taste immortality – both physical immortality and other sorts. (For immortals, of course, it's different.) So it's not surprising that everything naturally values its own offspring. They all feel this concern, and this love, because of their desire for immortality.'

I found these ideas totally novel, and I said, 'Well, Diotima, that's a very clever explanation. Is it really all true?' And she, in her best lecturer's manner, replied, 'There can be no question of it. Take another human characteristic, ambition. It seems absurdly irrational until you remember my explanation. Think of the extraordinary behaviour of those who, prompted by Eros, are eager to become famous, and "amass undying fame for the whole of time to come". For this they will expose themselves to danger even more than they will for their children. They will spend money, endure any hardship, even die for it. Think of Alcestis' willingness to die for Admetus, or Achilles' determination to follow Patroclus in death, or your Athenian king Codrus and his readiness to give up his life for his children's right to rule. Would they have done these things if they hadn't thought they were leaving behind them an undying memory which we still possess – of their courage? Of course not. The desire for undying nobility, and the good reputation which goes with it, is a universal human motive. The nobler people are, the more strongly they feel it. They desire immortality.

'Those whose creative urge is physical tend to turn to women, and pursue Eros by this route. The production of children gains them, as they imagine, immortality and a name and happiness for themselves, for all time. In others the impulse is mental or spiritual – people who are creative mentally, much more than physically. They produce what you would expect the mind to conceive and produce. And what is that? Thought, and all other human excellence. All poets are creators of this kind, and so are those artists who are generally regarded as inventive. However, under the general heading "thought", by far the finest and most important item is the art of political and domestic economy, what we call good judgement, and justice.

'Someone who, right from his youth, is mentally creative in these areas, when he is ready, and the time comes, feels a strong urge to give birth, or beget. So he goes around, like everyone else, searching, as I see it, for a medium of beauty in which he can create. He will never create in an ugly medium. So in his desire to create he is attracted to what is physically beautiful rather than ugly. But if he comes across a beautiful, noble, well-formed mind, then he finds the combination particularly attractive. He'll drop everything and embark on long conversations about goodness, with such a companion,

c trying to teach him about the nature and behaviour of the good man. Now that he's made contact with someone beautiful, and made friends with him, he can produce and bring to birth what he long ago conceived. Present or absent, he keeps it in mind, and joins with his friends in bringing his conception to maturity. In consequence such people have a far stronger bond between them than there is between the parents of children; and they form much firmer friendships, because they are jointly responsible for finer, and more lasting, offspring.

'We would all choose children of this kind for ourselves, rather than human children. We look

d with envy at Homer and Hesiod, and the other great poets, and the marvellous progeny they left behind, which have brought them undying fame and memory: or, if you like, at children of the kind which Lycurgus left in Sparta, the salvation of Sparta and practically all Greece. In your city, Solon is highly thought of, as the father of your laws, as are many

e other men in other states, both Greek and foreign. They have published to the world a variety of noble achievements, and created goodness of every kind. There are shrines to such people in honour of their offspring, but none to the producers of ordinary children.

'You, too, Socrates, could probably be initiated this far into knowledge of Eros. But all this, rightly

210 pursued, is a mere preliminary to the full rites, and final revelation, which might well be beyond you.

Still, I'll tell you about it, so that if I fail, it won't be for want of trying. Try to follow if you can.

'The true follower of this subject must begin, as a young man, with the pursuit of physical beauty. In the first place, if his mentor advises him properly, he should be attracted, physically, to one individual; at this stage his offspring are beautiful discussions and conversations. Next he should realize that the physical beauty of one body is akin to that of any other body, and that if he's going to pursue beauty of appearance, it's the height of folly not to regard the beauty which is in all bodies as one and the same. This insight will convert him into a lover of all physical beauty, and he will become less obsessive in his pursuit of his one former passion, as he realizes its unimportance.

'The next stage is to put a higher value on mental than on physical beauty. The right qualities of mind, even in the absence of any great physical beauty, will be enough to awaken his love and affection. He will generate the kind of discussions which are improving to the young. The aim is that, as the next step, he should be compelled to contemplate the beauty of customs and institutions, to see that all beauty of this sort is related, and consequently to regard physical beauty as trivial.

'From human institutions his teacher should direct him to knowledge, so that he may, in turn, see the beauty of different types of knowledge. Whereas before, in servile and contemptible fashion, he was dominated by the individual case, loving the beauty of a boy, or a man, or a single human activity, now he directs his eyes to what is beautiful in general, as he turns to gaze upon the limitless ocean of beauty. Now he produces many fine and inspiring thoughts and arguments, as he gives his undivided attention to philosophy. Here he gains in strength and stature until his attention is caught by that one special knowledge – the knowledge of a beauty which I will now try to describe to you. So pay the closest possible attention.

'When a man has reached this point in his education in love, studying the different types of beauty in correct order, he will come to the final end and goal of this education. Then suddenly he will see a beauty of a breathtaking nature, Socrates, the beauty which is the justification of all his efforts so far. It is eternal, neither coming to be nor passing away, neither increasing nor decreasing. Moreover it is not beautiful in part and ugly in part, nor is it beautiful at one time and not at another; nor beautiful in some respects but not in others; nor beautiful here and ugly there, as if beautiful in some people's eyes but not in others. It will not appear to him as the beauty of a face, or hands, or anything physical – nor as an idea or branch of knowledge, nor as existing in any determinate place, such as a living creature, or the earth, or heaven, or anywhere like that. It exists for all time, by itself and with itself, unique. All other forms of beauty derive from it, but in such a way that their creation or destruction does not strengthen or weaken it, or affect it in any way at all. If a man progresses (as he will do, if he goes about his love affairs in the right way) from the lesser beauties, and begins to catch sight of this beauty, then he is within reach of the final revelation. Such is the experience of the man who approaches, or is guided towards, love in the right way, beginning with the particular examples of beauty, but always returning from them to the search for that one beauty. He uses them like a ladder, climbing from the love of one person to love of two; from two to love of all physical beauty; from physical beauty to beauty in human behaviour; thence to beauty in subjects of study; from them he arrives finally at that branch of knowledge which studies nothing but ultimate beauty. Then at last he understands what true beauty is.

'That, if ever, is the moment, my dear Socrates, when a man's life is worth living, as he contemplates beauty itself. Once seen, it will not seem to you to be a good such as gold, or fashionable clothes, or the boys and young men who have such an effect on you now when you see them. You, and any number of people like you, when you see your boy-friends and spend all your time with them, are quite prepared (or would be, if it were possible) to go without food and drink, just looking at them and being with them. But suppose it were granted to someone to see beauty itself quite clearly, in its pure, undiluted form – not clogged up with human flesh and colouring, and a whole lot of other worthless and corruptible matter. No, imagine he were able to see the divine beauty itself in its unique essence. Don't you think he would find it a wonderful way to live, looking at it, contemplating it as it should be contemplated, and spending his time in its company? It cannot fail to strike you that only then will it be possible for him, seeing beauty as it should be

c

d

e

212

seen, to produce, not likenesses of goodness (since it is no likeness he has before him), but the real thing (since he has the real thing before him); and that this producing, and caring for, real goodness earns him the friendship of the gods and makes him, if anyone, immortal.'

b   There you are, then, Phaedrus and the rest of you. That's what Diotima said to me, and I, for one, find it convincing. And it's because I'm convinced that I now try to persuade other people as well that man, in his search for this goal, could hardly hope to find a better ally than Eros. That's why I say that everyone should honour Eros, and why I myself honour him, and make the pursuit of Eros my chief concern, and encourage others to do the same. Now, and for all time, I praise the power and vigour of Eros, to the limits of my ability.

c   That's my speech, Phaedrus. You can take it, if you like, as a formal eulogy of Eros. Or you can call it by any other name you please.

This speech was greeted with applause, and Aristophanes started saying something about Socrates' reference to his speech, when suddenly there was a tremendous sound of hammering at the front door – people going home from a party, by the sound of it. You could hear the voice of a flute girl.

d   AGATHON [*to his slaves*]: Could you see who that is? If it's one of my friends, ask him in. Otherwise, say we've stopped drinking and are just going to bed.

Almost at once we heard Alcibiades' voice from the courtyard. He was very drunk, and shouting at the top of his voice, asking 'where Agathon was', and demanding 'to be taken to Agathon'. So in he came, supported by the girl, and some of his followers. He stood there in the doorway, wearing a luxuriant garland of ivy and violets, with his head covered in ribbons.

ALCIBIADES: Greetings, gentlemen. Will you allow me to join your gathering completely drunk? Or shall we just crown Agathon (which is what we've come for) and go away? I couldn't come yesterday, but now here I am, with ribbons in my hair, so that I can take a garland from my own head, and crown the man whom I hereby proclaim the cleverest and handsomest man in Athens. Are you going to laugh at me for being drunk? Well, you may laugh, but I'm sure I'm right, all the same. Anyway, those are my terms. So tell me right away: should I come in? Will you drink with me, or not?

Then everyone started talking at once, telling him to come in and sit down. And Agathon called him over. So over he came, assisted by his companions. He was taking off his ribbons, getting ready to put the garland on Agathon, and with the ribbons in front of his eyes he didn't see Socrates. So he sat down next to Agathon, between him and Socrates, Socrates moving aside, when he saw him, to make room. As he sat down he greeted Agathon, and put the garland on his head.

AGATHON [*to his slaves*]: Take Alcibiades' shoes off. He can make a third at this table.

ALCIBIADES: Excellent, but who is the other person drinking at our table? [*turning and seeing Socrates, and leaping to his feet*] My God, what's this? Socrates here? You've been lying in wait here for c me, just as you used to do. You were always turning up unexpectedly, wherever I least expected you. What are you doing here this time? And come to that, how've you managed to get yourself a place next to the most attractive person in the room? You ought to be next to someone like Aristophanes; he sets out to make himself ridiculous, and succeeds. Shouldn't you be with him?

SOCRATES: I'm going to need your protection, Agathon. I've found the love of this man a bit of a nightmare. From the day I took a fancy to him, I d haven't been allowed to look at, or talk to, anyone attractive at all. If I do he gets envious and jealous, and starts behaving outrageously. He insults me, and can barely keep his hands off me. So you make sure he doesn't do anything now. You reconcile us, or defend me if he resorts to violence. His insane sexuality scares me stiff.

ALCIBIADES: There can be no reconciliation between you and me. However, I'll get my revenge another time. For the moment, give me some of those ribbons, Agathon, so I can make a garland e for this remarkable head of his as well. I don't want him complaining that I crowned you, and not him, though he is the international grandmaster of words – and not just the day before yesterday, like you, but all the time. [*As he said this he took some of the ribbons, made a garland for Socrates, and sat down.*] Well, gentlemen, you seem to me to be pretty sober. We can't have that. You'll have to drink. After all, that's what we agreed. So I'm going to choose a Master of Ceremonies, to see you all get enough to drink. I choose myself. Agathon, let them bring a large cup, if you've got one. No, wait! [*Suddenly catching sight of an ice-bucket holding upwards of half a gallon.*] No need for that. Boy, bring me that ice-bucket. [*He filled it, and started off by draining it himself. Then he told the slave to fill it up again for Socrates.*] A useless ploy against Socrates, gentlemen. It doesn't matter how much you give him to drink, he'll drink it and be none the worse for wear. [*So the slave filled the bucket for Socrates, who drank it.*]

214

ERYXIMACHUS: What's the plan, Alcibiades? Are we just going to sit here and drink as if we were dying of thirst? Aren't we going to talk, or sing, at all while we drink?

b

ALCIBIADES: Ah, Eryximachus. Most excellent scion of a most excellent and sensible father. Good evening.

ERYXIMACHUS: Good evening to you too. But what *do* you want us to do?

ALCIBIADES: Whatever you recommend. We must do as you say. After all, 'a doctor is worth a dozen ordinary men'. So you tell us your prescription.

ERYXIMACHUS: Very well, listen. We had decided, before you came, that going round anti-clockwise, each of us in turn should make the best speech he could about Eros, in praise of him. We've all made our speeches. You've drunk but you haven't spoken. So it's only fair that you should speak now; after that you can give any instructions you like to Socrates, and he can do the same to the man on his right, and so on all the way round.

c

ALCIBIADES: That's a good idea, Eryximachus. But it's grossly unfair to ask me, drunk, to compete

with you sober. Also, my dear friend, I hope you
didn't pay any attention to Socrates' remarks just
now. Presumably you realize the situation is the
exact opposite of what he said. He's the one who
will resort to violence, if I praise anyone else, god
or man, in his presence.

SOCRATES: Can't you hold your tongue?

ALCIBIADES: Don't worry, I wouldn't dream of
praising anyone else if you're here.

ERYXIMACHUS: Well, that'll do, if you like.
Praise Socrates.

ALCIBIADES: Really? You think I should, Eryximachus? Shall I set about him, and get my own back
on him, here in front of you all?

SOCRATES: Hey! What are you up to? Trying to
make a fool of me by praising me? Or what?

ALCIBIADES: I'm going to tell the truth. Do you
mind that?

SOCRATES: Of course not. In fact, I'm all in
favour of it.

ALCIBIADES: I can't wait to start. And here's
what you can do. If I say anything that's not true,
you can interrupt me, if you like, and tell me I'm
wrong. I shan't get anything wrong on purpose, but
don't be surprised if my recollection of things is a
bit higgledy-piggledy. It's not easy, when you're as
drunk as I am, to give a clear and orderly account
of someone as strange as you.

ALCIBIADES

Gentlemen, I'm going to try and praise Socrates
using similes. He may think I'm trying to make a

fool of him, but the point of the simile is its accuracy, not its absurdity. I think he's very like one of those Silenus-figures sculptors have on their shelves. They're made with flutes or pipes. You can open them up, and when you do you find little figures of the gods inside. I also think Socrates is like the satyr Marsyas. As far as your appearance goes, Socrates, even you can't claim these are poor comparisons, but I'll tell you how the likeness holds good in other ways; just listen. You're a troublemaker, aren't you? Don't deny it, I can bring witnesses. You may not play the pipes, like Marsyas, but what you do is much more amazing. He had only to open his mouth to delight men, but he needed a musical instrument to do it. The same goes for anyone nowadays who plays his music — I count what Olympus played as really Marsyas', since he learned from him. His is the only music which carries people away, and reveals those who have a desire for the gods and their rites. Such is its divine power, and it makes no difference whether it's played by an expert, or by a mere flute girl.

You have the same effect on people. The only difference is that you do it with words alone, without the aid of any instrument. We can all listen to anyone else talking, and it has virtually no effect on us, no matter what he's talking about, or how good a speaker he is. But when we listen to you, or to someone else using your arguments, even if he's a hopeless speaker, we're overwhelmed and carried away. This is true of men, women and children alike.

For my own part, gentlemen, I would like to tell

you on my honour (only you would certainly think
I was drunk) the effect what he says has had on me
in the past – and still does have, to this day. When
I hear him, it's like the worst kind of religious hys-
teria. My heart pounds, and I find myself in floods
of tears, such is the effect of his words. And I can
tell lots of other people feel the same. I used to
listen to Pericles and other powerful speakers, and
I thought they spoke well. But they never had the
effect on me of turning all my beliefs upside down,
with the disturbing realization that my whole life is
that of a slave. Whereas this Marsyas here has often
made me feel that, and decide that the kind of life
I lead is just not worth living. You can't deny it,
Socrates.

Even now I know in my heart of hearts that if
I were to listen to him, I couldn't resist him. The
same thing would happen again. He forces me to
admit that with all my faults I do nothing to
improve myself, but continue in public life just the
same. So I tear myself away, as if stopping my ears
against the Sirens; otherwise I would spend my
whole life there sitting at his feet. He's the only
man who can appeal to my better nature (not that
most people would reckon I *had* a better nature),
because I'm only too aware I have no answer to
his arguments. I know I should do as he tells me,
but when I leave him I have no defence against
my own ambition and desire for recognition. So I
run for my life, and avoid him, and when I see him,
I'm embarrassed, when I remember conclusions
we've reached in the past. I would often cheerfully
have seen him dead, and yet I know that if that

did happen, I should be even more upset. So I just   c
can't cope with the man.

I'm by no means the only person to be affected
like this by his satyr's music, but that isn't all I have
to say about his similarity to those figures I likened
him to, and about his remarkable powers. Believe
me, none of you really knows the man. So I'll
enlighten you, now that I've begun.

Your view of Socrates is of someone who fancies   d
attractive men, spends all his time with them, finds
them irresistible – and you know how hopelessly
ignorant and uncertain he is. And yet this pose is
extremely Silenus-like. It's the outward mask he
wears, like the carved Silenus. Open him up, and
he's a model of restraint – you wouldn't believe it,
my dear fellow-drinkers. Take my word for it, it
makes no difference at all how attractive you are;
he has an astonishing contempt for that kind of
thing. Similarly with riches, or any of the other so-   e
called advantages we possess. He regards all possessions as worthless, and us humans as insignificant.
No, I mean it – he treats his whole life in human
society as a game or puzzle.

But when he's serious, when he opens up and
you see the real Socrates – I don't know if any of
you has ever seen the figure inside. I saw it once,
and it struck me as utterly godlike and golden and   217
beautiful and wonderful. In fact, I thought I must
simply do anything he told me. And since I thought
he was serious about my good looks, I congratu-
lated myself on a fantastic stroke of luck, which
had given me the chance to satisfy Socrates, and
be the recipient, in return, of all his knowledge.

I had, I may say, an extremely high opinion of my own looks.

That was my plan, so I did what I had never done up to then – I sent away my attendant, and took to seeing him on my own. You see, I'm going to tell you the whole truth, so listen carefully, and you tell them, Socrates, if I get anything wrong. Well, gentlemen, I started seeing him – just the two of us – and I thought he would start talking to me as lovers do to their boyfriends when they're alone together. I was very excited. But nothing like that happened at all. He spent the day talking to me as usual, and then left. I invited him to the gymnasium with me, and exercised with him there, thinking I might make some progress that way. So he exercised and wrestled with me, often completely on our own, and (needless to say) it got me nowhere at all. When that turned out to be no good, I thought I'd better make a pretty determined assault on the man, and not give up, now that I'd started. I wanted to find out what the trouble was. So I asked him to dinner, just like a lover with designs on his boyfriend.

He took some time to agree even to this, but finally I did get him to come. The first time he came, he had dinner, and then got up to go. I lost my nerve, that time, and let him go. But I decided to try again. He came to dinner, and I kept him talking late into the night. When he tried to go home, I made him stay, saying it was too late to go. So he stayed the night on the couch next to mine. There was no one else sleeping in the room.

What I've told you so far I'd be quite happy to

repeat to anyone. The next part I'm only telling you because (a) I'm drunk – '*in vino veritas*', and all that – and (b) since I've started praising Socrates, it seems wrong to leave out an example of his superior behaviour. Besides, I'm like someone who's been bitten by an adder. They say that a man who's had this happen to him will only say what it was like to others who've been bitten; they're the only people who will understand, and make allowances for, his willingness to say or do anything, such is the pain. Well, I've been bitten by something worse than an adder, and in the worst possible place. I've been stung, or bitten, in my heart or soul (whatever you care to call it) by a method of philosophical argument, whose bite, when it gets a grip on a young and intelligent mind, is sharper than any adder's. It makes one willing to say or do anything. I can see all these Phaedruses and Agathons, Eryximachuses, Pausaniases, Aristodemuses and Aristophaneses here, not to mention Socrates himself and the rest of you. You've all had a taste of this wild passion for philosophy, so you'll understand me, and forgive what I did then, and what I'm telling you now. As for the servants, and anyone else who's easily shocked, or doesn't know what I'm talking about, they'll just have to put something over their ears.

218

b

There we were, then, gentlemen. The lamp had gone out, the slaves had gone to bed. I decided it was time to abandon subtlety, and say plainly what I was after. So I nudged him. 'Socrates, are you asleep?' 'No.' 'Do you know what I've decided?' 'What?' 'I think you're the ideal person to be my

c

lover, but you seem to be a bit shy about suggesting it. So I'll tell you how I feel about it. I think I'd be crazy not to satisfy you in this way, just as I'd do anything else for you if it was in my power – or in

d   my friends' power. Nothing matters more to me than my own improvement, and I can't imagine a better helper than you. Anyone with any sense would think worse of me for not giving a man like you what he wants than most ignorant people would if I did give you what you want.'

Socrates listened to this. Then, with character-istic irony, he replied. 'My dear Alcibiades, you're certainly nobody's fool, if you're right in what you

e   say about me, and I do have some power to improve you. It must be remarkable beauty you see in me, far superior to your own physical beauty. If that's the aim of your deal with me, to exchange beauty for beauty, then you're trying to get much the better of the bargain. You want to get real beauty in exchange for what is commonly mistaken for it, like

219   Diomedes getting gold armour in return for his bronze. Better think again, however. You might be wrong about me. Judgement begins when eyesight starts to fail, and you're still a long way from that.'

I listened, then said: 'Well, as far as I am con-cerned, that's how things stand. I've told you my real feelings. You must decide what you think best for yourself and for me.' 'That's good advice. We

b   must think about it some time, and act as seems best to us, in this matter as in others.'

After this exchange, thinking my direct assault had made some impact, I got up, before he could say anything more, wrapped my cloak around him

(it was winter), and lay down with him under his
rough cloak. I put my arms round him. I spent
the whole night with him, remarkable, superhuman   c
being that he is – still telling the truth, Socrates,
you can't deny it – but he was more than equal to
my advances. He rejected them, laughed at my good
looks, and treated them with contempt; and I must
admit that, as far as looks went, I thought I was
quite something, members of the jury. (I call you
that, since I'm accusing Socrates of contempt.) In
short, I promise you faithfully, I fell asleep, and
when I woke up in the morning I'd slept with
Socrates all night, but absolutely nothing had
happened. It was just like sleeping with one's father   d
or elder brother.

Imagine how I felt after that. I was humiliated
and yet full of admiration for Socrates' character
– his restraint and strength of mind. I'd met a man
whose equal, in intelligence and control, I didn't
think I should ever meet again. I couldn't have a
row with him; that would just lose me his friendship. Nor could I see any way of attracting him. I   e
knew money would make as little impression on
him as Trojan weapons on Ajax, and he'd already
escaped my one sure means of ensnaring him. I
didn't know what to do, and I went around infatuated with the man. No one's ever been so
infatuated.

That was the background to our military service
together in Potidaea, where we were messmates. In
the first place there was his toughness – not only
greater than mine, but greater than anyone else's.
Sometimes we were cut off and had to go without

220 food, as happens on campaign. No one could match him for endurance. On the other hand, he was the one who really made the most of it when there was plenty. He wouldn't drink for choice, but if he had to, he drank us all under the table. Surprising as it may seem, no man has ever seen Socrates drunk. I've no doubt you'll see confirmation of that this evening. As for the weather (they have pretty savage winters up there), his indifference to it was always astonishing, but one occasion stands out in particular.

b There was an incredibly severe frost. No one went outside, or if they did, they went muffled up to the eyeballs, with their feet wrapped up in wool or sheepskin. In these conditions Socrates went out in the same cloak he always wore, and walked barefoot over the ice with less fuss than the rest of us who had our feet wrapped up. The men didn't like it at all; they thought he was getting at them.

c So much for that. But there's another exploit of this 'conquering hero' during that campaign, which I ought to tell you about. He was studying a problem one morning, and he stood there thinking about it, not making any progress, but not giving up either – just standing there, trying to find the answer. By midday people were beginning to take notice, and to remark to one another in some surprise that Socrates had been standing there thinking since dawn. Finally, in the evening after supper, some of

d the Ionians brought out their mattresses (this was in summer), and slept in the open, keeping an eye on him to see if he'd stand there all night. And sure enough he did stand there, until dawn broke and the sun rose. Then he said a prayer to the sun and left.

Should I say something about his conduct in action? Yes, I think he's earned it. In the battle in which the generals gave me a decoration, my own life was saved by none other than Socrates. He refused to leave me when I was wounded, and saved both me and my weapons. So I recommended that the generals should give you the decoration. Isn't that true, Socrates? You can't object to that, or say I'm lying, can you? In fact the generals were inclined to favour me, because of my social position, and wanted to give it to me, but you were keener than they were that I should get it, rather than you.

And you should have seen him, gentlemen, on the retreat from Delium. I was with him, but I was on horseback, and he was on foot. He was retreating, amid the general rout, with Laches. I came upon them, and when I saw them I told them not to panic, and said I'd stick by them. This time I got a better view of Socrates than I had at Potidaea, since I was on horseback, and less worried about my own safety. For a start, he was much more composed than Laches. And then I thought your description of him, Aristophanes, was as accurate there as it is here in Athens, 'marching along with his head in the air, staring at all around him', calmly contemplating friend and foe alike. It was perfectly clear, even from a distance, that any attempt to lay a finger on him would arouse vigorous resistance. So he and his companion escaped unhurt. On the whole, in battle, you don't meddle with people like that. You go after the ones in headlong flight.

I could go on praising Socrates all night, and tell you some surprising things. Many of his qualities

e

221

b

c

can be found in other people, and yet it's remarkable
how unlike he is to anyone in the past or present.
You can compare Brasidas, or someone like that,
with Achilles; Pericles with Nestor or Antenor (for
example); and make other similar comparisons. But
you could go a long way and not find a match,
dead or living, for Socrates. So unusual are the man
himself and his arguments. You have to go back to
my original comparison of the man and his arguments, to Silenuses and satyrs. I didn't say this at
the beginning, but his arguments, when you really
look at them, are also just like Silenus-figures. If
you decided to listen to one, it would strike you at
first as ludicrous. On the face of it, it's just a collection of irrelevant words and phrases, but those are
just the outer skin of this trouble-making satyr. It's
all donkeys and bronzesmiths, shoemakers and tanners. He always seems to be repeating himself, and
people who haven't heard him before, and aren't
too quick on the uptake, laugh at what he says. But
look beneath the surface, and get inside them, and
you'll find two things. In the first place, they're the
only arguments which really make any sense; on
top of that they are supremely inspiring, because
they contain countless models of excellence and
pointers towards it. In fact, they deal with everything you should be concerned about if you want
to lead a good and noble life.

That's my speech, gentlemen, in praise of Socrates – though I've included a bit of blame as well
for his outrageous treatment of me. And I'm not
the only sufferer. There's Charmides, the son of
Glaucon, and Euthydemus, the son of Diocles, and

lots of others. He seduces them, like a lover seducing his boyfriend, and then it turns out he's not their lover at all; in fact, they're his lovers. So take my advice, Agathon, and don't be seduced. Learn from our experience, rather than at first hand, like Homer's 'fool who learned too late'. Don't trust him an inch.

Alcibiades' candour aroused some amusement. He seemed to be still in love with Socrates. c

SOCRATES: Not so drunk after all, Alcibiades; or you wouldn't have avoided, so elegantly and so deviously, revealing the real object of your speech, just slipping it in at the end, as if it were an afterthought. What you're really trying to do is turn Agathon and me against one another. You think that I should be your lover, and no one else's; and that you, and no one else, should be Agathon's. Well, it hasn't worked. All that stuff about satyrs and Silenuses is quite transparent. You mustn't let him get away with it, my dear Agathon; you must make sure no one turns us against each other. d

AGATHON: You may be right, Socrates. His sitting between us, to keep us apart, bears that out. But it won't work. I'll come round and sit next to you. e

SOCRATES: Good idea. Sit here, round this side.

ALCIBIADES: Ye gods. What I have to put up with from the man. He has to keep scoring off me. Look, at least let Agathon sit in the middle.

SOCRATES: Out of the question. You've just praised me, and now I must praise the person on my right. If Agathon sits next to you, he can't be expected to make *another* speech in praise of me. I'd better make one in praise of him instead. No, you'll

223   have to admit defeat, my good friend, and put up with me praising the boy. I look forward to it.

    AGATHON: What a bit of luck. I'm certainly not staying here, Alcibiades. I'd much rather move, and get myself praised by Socrates.

    ALCIBIADES: That's it, the same old story. Whenever Socrates is around, no one else can get near anyone good-looking. Like now, for example. Look how easily he finds plausible reasons why Agathon should sit next to him.

b   Agathon got up to come and sit by Socrates. Suddenly a whole crowd of people on their way home from a party turned up at the door, and finding it open (someone was just leaving), they came straight in, and sat down to join us. Things became incredibly noisy and disorderly, and we couldn't avoid having far too much to drink. Eryximachus and Phaedrus and some others went home. I fell

c asleep, and slept for some time, the nights being long at that time of year. When I woke up it was almost light, and the cocks were crowing. I could see that everyone had gone home or to sleep, apart from Agathon, Aristophanes and Socrates. They were still awake and drinking (passing a large bowl round anti-clockwise). Socrates was holding the floor. I've forgotten most of what he was saying,

d since I missed the beginning of it, and was still half-asleep anyway. The gist of it was that he was forcing them to admit that the same man could be capable of writing comedy and tragedy, and hence that a successful tragedian must also be able to write comedy. As they were being driven to this conclusion, though not really following the argument, they dropped off. Aristophanes went to sleep first, and then, as it was getting light, Agathon. Socrates made them both comfortable, and got up to leave himself. I followed him, as usual. He went to the Lyceum, had a bath, spent the rest of the day as he normally would, and then, towards evening, went home to bed.

PHAEDRUS

SOCRATES: Hello, Phaedrus. Where are you going, and what have you been up to?

PHAEDRUS: I'm going for a walk in the country, Socrates. And I've been with Lysias, the son of Cephalus. I spent some time there – in fact, I've been sitting there since sunrise. So I'm taking the advice of Acumenus, who is a friend of yours and mine, and going for a walk on the country roads. He says it's better for you than walking in the covered ways. b

SOCRATES: He's right, my friend. So Lysias was in the city, then.

PHAEDRUS: Yes, at Epicrates' house, near the temple of Olympian Zeus. Where Morychus used to live.

SOCRATES: And what were you doing? Lysias was regaling you with his speeches, no doubt.

PHAEDRUS: I'll tell you, if you've got time to walk with me and hear what I've got to say.

SOCRATES: Of course I have. You must be aware that I count it, in Pindar's phrase, 'more precious than time itself' to hear what you and Lysias have been up to.

PHAEDRUS: Come on, then. Lead the way. c

SOCRATES: And you tell me about it.

PHAEDRUS: I will. It's an ideal topic for you,

Socrates, because the speech we were interested in was about love, though in a rather unusual way. The subject of Lysias' speech is someone good-looking being solicited – but not by a lover. Indeed, that's why the speech is such a *tour de force*. He should grant his favours, Lysias says, to a man who is not his lover, in preference to one who is.

SOCRATES: Good for Lysias. A pity he didn't say to a poor man in preference to a rich, to an older man rather than a younger, or in general to people

d   like me and the rest of us. Then his speech really would be an accomplished and public-spirited piece of work. I can't wait to hear it. So even if your walk takes you to Megara and back, setting foot on the wall as Herodicus recommends, I'm certainly not going to be left behind.

PHAEDRUS: For heaven's sake, Socrates! Lysias

228 is the cleverest speech-writer alive today. He's had a long time to think about this speech and compose it. Are you suggesting that an amateur like me can recall it in a way that does justice to him? No chance – though I'd give a small fortune to be able to.

SOCRATES: Listen, Phaedrus. If I don't know my Phaedrus, then I have lost all memory of myself as well. But I do, and I haven't. If he heard a speech of Lysias, I'm quite sure he didn't just listen to it once. I've no doubt he kept on pestering him to recite it, and Lysias was happy enough to do so. But

b   even this wasn't enough for Phaedrus. In the end he borrowed the book, and started taking a closer look at the bits he couldn't resist. He sat there doing this from sunrise, and then when he'd had enough, he went for a walk. Ye dogs! I wouldn't mind betting he actually knows the speech by heart, unless it was a really long one. And he was taking his walk outside the city so that he could rehearse it. But then he met a man with a weakness for listening to speeches; and seeing him, he was delighted with the sight, because it meant he would have a companion in his state of ecstasy. 'Come on. Lead the way,' he said to him. But when the lover of speeches asked him to deliver the speech, he went all coy, as if he didn't want to. And yet he did mean to speak in the end, even if he had to force the speech on his listener against his will. So why don't you ask him, Phaedrus, to do here and now what he has every intention of doing fairly soon anyway?

PHAEDRUS: I really think the best thing will be for me to deliver the speech as well as I can. It looks as if you're not going to let me go until, one way or another, I do speak.

SOCRATES: Quite right. I'm not.

PHAEDRUS: Very well. That's what I'll do. Seriously, Socrates, I promise you, I didn't learn it by heart. But I can give you a general idea of pretty well all the ways in which he said the lover's claim differed from that of the non-lover. I'll give you a summary of each point in turn, starting at the beginning.

SOCRATES: Yes, do. Only first, my friend, please show me what it is you have there under your cloak, in your left hand. My guess is it's the speech itself you've got there. If it is, be under no illusions about what I want. Much as I love you, I have no intention whatever of being your guinea-pig, if Lysias is here in person. Come on, let's have a look.

PHAEDRUS: All right, that's enough. I was hoping for a quick workout with you, Socrates. But you've cheated me of that hope. Let's sit down and read it. Where shall we go?

229 SOCRATES: Let's turn off here. We can walk along the Ilissus, and sit down in some quiet spot, wherever we like.

PHAEDRUS: Lucky I'm not wearing shoes, by the looks of it. Of course you never do anyway. So there's nothing to stop us following the stream, with our feet in the water. It'll be refreshing, too, at this time of year, and this time of day.

SOCRATES: After you, then. Keep an eye open for somewhere we can sit down.

PHAEDRUS: What about over there – you see that enormous plane tree?

SOCRATES: I do.

b PHAEDRUS: There's shade there, and a nice bit of breeze, and grass to sit on, or lie on, if we'd rather.

SOCRATES: Lead on.

PHAEDRUS: Tell me, Socrates, wasn't it somewhere round here by the Ilissus that Boreas is said to have carried off Oreithuia?

SOCRATES: Yes, it was.

PHAEDRUS: Was this the place? The water seems lovely and clean and clear – just the place for girls to be playing.

c SOCRATES: No, it was further down, about quarter of a mile or so, where you cross over to get to Agra. There's some sort of shrine there, to Boreas.

PHAEDRUS: I've never really noticed. Seriously,

though, Socrates, when you come across a legend of that sort, do you really believe it to be true?

SOCRATES: I'd be in good company if I didn't. I could say, like any good rationalist, that she was playing on the rocks nearby, with Pharmaceia, and that a gust of wind made her overbalance. And because she met her death in this way, in time it came to be said that she'd been carried off by Boreas. Or maybe it was on the Areopagus. That's another version of the story, that she was carried off from there, not from here. Personally, Phaedrus, I find that sort of explanation quite appealing up to a point, but a bit too ingenious and painstaking. And I feel a bit sorry for its propounder, if only because he then has no choice but to put us right on the appearance of the Centaurs, and then of course the Chimaera, and then he's overwhelmed by a whole crowd of similar creatures: Gorgons, Pegasuses, and a huge number of bizarre mythical beasts which are impossible to explain away. A sceptic, trying to reduce all of these to what is probable, will find his clumsy rationalism making huge demands on his time. I simply haven't the time for all that. And the reason, my friend, is this. I haven't so far succeeded in following the Delphic dictum to 'know myself', and for as long as I still don't know about myself, it strikes me as absurd to be enquiring into things which are nothing to do with me. That's why I pay no attention to them, and accept the conventional beliefs about them, as I said just now. The object of my enquiry is not those things, but rather myself. Am I really a wild beast, more complex and violent than Typhon, or a gentler and simpler creature, endowed by nature with some superhuman quality quite unlike Typhon?

However, to interrupt our discussion, my friend, wasn't this the tree you were taking us to?

b   PHAEDRUS: The very one.

SOCRATES: What a truly delightful place to rest! This tall, spreading plane tree – and the agnus, what wonderful height and shade! And it's in full flower. What a wonderful smell! And how charming the stream is, flowing beneath the plane. And beautifully cool, if my foot is a reliable witness. Judging by the figurines and statuettes, it looks as if the place is sacred to Achelous and some of the

c   Nymphs. Or again, if you prefer, there's the freshness of the place. How pleasant it is – quite delightful, in fact. And the shrill summer song of the cicadas – how clearly it echoes. But above all the grass. A perfect choice. On this gentle slope, it makes an excellent cushion for the head, if you want to lie down. I couldn't have asked for a better guide, Phaedrus.

PHAEDRUS: Socrates, you amaze me. I find you quite extraordinary. You really do seem like a tourist, as you suggest, and not like a local. That's what

d   comes of never going abroad – or even, as far as I can see, setting foot outside the city at all.

SOCRATES: Be patient with me, my friend. I'm a lover of learning. The countryside and the trees aren't going to teach me anything – only the people in the city. All the same, I think you've found the recipe for getting me out. Like someone getting a hungry animal to move by dangling a fresh shoot or vegetable in front of it. That's what you're doing

to me, dangling books of speeches under my nose
like this. It looks as if you're going to take me on a
conducted tour of Attica – and anywhere else that
takes your fancy.

Anyway, here we are. And now that I've got here,
I think I'll lie down. As for you, find the best position you can for reading and read to me.

PHAEDRUS: Very well. Listen.

'You know how things are with me, and you have
heard me explain why I think it would be a good
thing for us that this should happen. I don't think
the fact of my not being your lover should stop me
getting what I want. Lovers, when their desire
cools, regret the benefits they have conferred. But
for those who are not lovers, no time of regret
arises. They are not compelled to confer benefits;
they do it freely, with an eye to their own best
interests, within the limits of their ability. Then
again, lovers look at the mess their love has caused
them to make of their own affairs, and the benefits
they have conferred; adding to that the hardships
they have put up with, they reckon they have long
since made adequate payment to those they love.
Those who are not in love cannot plead neglect
of their own affairs; they cannot keep account of
hardships they have suffered in the past, nor blame
their love for quarrels with their family. They are
free of these troubles. All they have to do is concentrate on doing the things they think will give most
pleasure to the other party.

'Another reason put forward for preferring
lovers is that they are the truest friends to those
they love. They say they are prepared, in word and

e

231

b

c

deed alike, to offend the rest of the world in order to gratify their boyfriends. If they are telling the truth, you can easily see that they will put a still higher value on the next person they fall in love with; clearly they will treat the previous loved one badly if that is what the new one decrees. Then again, what can be the sense in giving something of this value to someone who is suffering from an affliction which anyone who knows anything about it will agree is incurable? After all, the sufferers themselves admit that they are ill, that they are not thinking straight. They say they know they are not in their right minds, that they have lost control of themselves. How can you expect them, when they do start thinking straight again, to regard as right the decisions they made when they were in that state? What is more, if you chose the best from among your lovers, you wouldn't have very many to choose from, whereas choosing the one who best suits you out of all the others gives you a wide choice. There is a much greater likelihood, among the many, of finding the man who is worthy of your friendship.

'You may be worried about public opinion, afraid you will be criticized when people find out. Well, the chances are that those who are in love will get a kick out of talking about it, expecting the congratulations of others to be added to their own. It will be a matter of pride to them to demonstrate to the world that all their hard work has not been for nothing. Those who are not in love, having more control over themselves, will prefer what is best to the good opinion of the world. Again, it is inevitable, if lovers follow the ones they love around and make a great thing of it, that a large number of people will see and hear about it. Whenever they are seen talking to one another, people think they have just been satisfying, or are just about to satisfy, their desires, and that that is why they are together. It wouldn't occur to them to censure those who are *not* in love for being together. They know that conversation is essential both to friendship and to other pleasures.

'What is more, you may be alarmed at the thought that friendship does not easily endure, and that while in the normal course of events a quarrel constitutes an equally great misfortune for both parties, in this case it is you who will be most harmed, since you have given away that which you value most highly. If that is what you are afraid of, there is good reason to fear lovers more. Lovers can take offence at all sorts of things; they think everything that happens is done to injure them. That is why they discourage the ones they love from meeting other people. They are worried that those who possess property may outbid them, and that those who have an education may turn out to be intellectually superior. As for people possessing any other good quality, they are invariably wary of their influence. So they persuade you to alienate these people, and reduce you to a state of friendlessness; and if you think about what is best for you, and show more sense than they do, you will fall out with them. But those who are not in fact in love, those who have got what they wanted on merit, would not object to people wanting to be with you. The ones they would resent would be those who refused your company; they would think they were despised by them, whereas they would regard the presence of those who did want your company as a help. The result is that the boy is much more likely to gain friends than enemies from the affair.

'Furthermore, many of those in love desire a boy's body before getting to know what he is like, or becoming familiar with his character in general. So it is not clear to them whether they will still want to be friends when their desire passes. Those who are not in love, on the other hand, were friends with each other even before they did the deed. It is unlikely their friendship will diminish as a result of benefits received; much more likely that these will remain as a reminder of benefits to come. As for your own improvement, you should be better off listening to me than to a lover. Lovers praise what you say and do even when it runs counter to what is best – sometimes through fear of losing your affection, sometimes because their own judgement is impaired by their desire. Look at the way love reveals itself in practice: if things go badly, it causes them to find fault with things which trouble no one else. If things go well, then even what gives no cause for pleasure inevitably evokes praise from them. As a result, there is far more reason for the ones they love to pity them than to admire them.

'If you take my advice, you will bear two points in mind. First, I don't just want your company with an eye to immediate pleasure, but also to future advantage. I am not overcome by love; I am master of myself. I shall not start a violent quarrel for some trivial reason; my anger, even when fully justified, will be mild and slow to arouse. I shall forgive unintentional offences, and try to sidestep intentional ones. These are the marks of a long-term friendship. If you still have it in your head that there can be no strong affection except from a man who really is in love, bear in mind that if this were so, we should not have any great regard for our sons, nor for our fathers and mothers; we should have no true friends – who have become our friends not out of this kind of desire, but from other shared interests.

'Again, if those in need have the strongest claim to be rewarded, then this ought to become a general principle: we should help, not the best people, but those most in need. The greater the hardship from which they are set free, the greater the gratitude they will feel. Furthermore, when entertaining privately, we should not invite our friends, but those who beg, and those who need a square meal. They, after all, are the people who will appreciate us and wait on us, who will call at our house, will feel the greatest pleasure, not to mention gratitude, and who will call down many blessings on our heads. No, I suspect it is better to grant favours, not to those whose need is greatest, but to those who are best able to repay them. Not those who are merely in love, but those who actually deserve what is on offer. Not those who will simply enjoy your youth and freshness, but those who, as you grow older, will share their strengths with you. Not those who, once they have done it, will boast about it to others, but those with a sense of decorum, those who will

d

e

234

keep quiet to all the world. Not those who are crazy about you in the short term, but those whose friendship will remain unaltered your whole life through. Not those who will look for an excuse for enmity once their desire starts to fade, but those who when you lose your youth and freshness, will then show their true worth. Remember my words, and keep one thing in mind: lovers receive lectures from their friends on the evils of being in love; no friend has ever yet blamed those who were not in love on the grounds that not being in love was against their best interests.

'In which case, you may ask, am I advising you to grant your favours to all those who are not in love with you? No, in my view even a lover would not advise you to adopt that attitude towards all your lovers. The man who gets you would have much less cause to be grateful, and you would not have the same ability to keep things secret from other people, if that was what you wanted. But the idea is that no harm should come of it, only benefit to both parties.

'I think I have said enough. But if you find there is something missing, if you think something has been left out, by all means ask.'

How does it strike you, Socrates, the speech? Don't you think it was in every way brilliant, particularly in its choice of language?

SOCRATES: It was out of this world, my friend. I am lost for words. And it was you, Phaedrus, who made me feel like that. I was watching you, and the speech seemed to make you come alive as you read it. 'Phaedrus knows about these things,' I thought to myself, 'and I don't.' So I followed you, and joined you in being carried away, since you were a man inspired.

PHAEDRUS: I see. Determined to make fun of it, then?

SOCRATES: Do you think I'm making fun of it? Aren't I in deadly earnest?

PHAEDRUS: Stop it, Socrates. Tell me honestly, e if you call yourself my friend, can you think of anyone else in Greece who could have made a stronger or lengthier speech on the same subject?

SOCRATES: What about praising the speech because we believe its author to have said what was right, and not just because it was clear and well-rounded, or beautifully turned in every phrase? Should we both be doing that as well? If we should, then I shall have to take your word for it. The speech lost me – my fault, I'm afraid. The only thing I was paying attention to was his powers of 235 persuasion. And as for those, even Lysias himself, I thought, regarded them as inadequate. He gave me the impression, Phaedrus, wouldn't you agree, of repeating himself once or twice. It was as if he felt he didn't have enough to make a long speech on the one theme – or perhaps he just wasn't very interested in it. A bit of youthful showing off, it struck me as, demonstrating that he was capable of saying the same thing in two quite different ways, and equally well in either way.

PHAEDRUS: You're wrong, Socrates. The speech b meets your requirements exactly. Whatever arguments worth mentioning the subject has to offer, he has included them all. Compared with what Lysias has said, no one could ever again make such a full or convincing speech.

SOCRATES: Now that is where I shall have to part company with you. If I decide to be obliging, and agree with you, the testimony of wise men and women of long ago – what they have said and written – will be against me.

c   PHAEDRUS: Which men and women? Where have you heard a better speech than this?

SOCRATES: I don't know that I can tell you that, straight out. I must have heard it somewhere – from the fair Sappho, perhaps, or the knowledgeable Anacreon, or somewhere in the prose writers. On what then do I rest my case? On a full heart, my friend. I feel I have things I could say which are quite different from Lysias' speech, and much better. I'm quite sure I didn't think of any of them for myself, since I'm only too aware how little I know. So the only other explanation is that I heard

d   about them – that I was filled up, like a jar – from some other source. But there again, in my stupid way, I've forgotten how and where I heard it.

PHAEDRUS: Now there's a good idea. Take no notice if I try and make you tell me where or how you heard it. Do just what you said. You have just promised to make a speech which is better than Lysias' book, no shorter, and quite different in content. I, in turn, promise you, like the nine archons, that I will match its weight with a golden statue at

e   Delphi. Not just of me, but one of you as well.

SOCRATES: You're a very dear friend, Phaedrus, pure gold through and through, if you take me to be saying that Lysias has missed the point completely, or that it is possible to make a speech without covering some of the same ground. I don't think that's something which could happen even to the worst of writers. Take the speech's theme, for a start — that you should grant your favours to the man who is not in love, in preference to the man who is. Can you imagine anyone speaking on that subject and not praising the good sense of the man who is not in love, and condemning the lover's lack of good sense? These are obvious points, after all. He can't leave them out and still have something original to say. No, in my opinion the speaker must be allowed and forgiven remarks of this kind. This is the kind of situation where we give marks for presentation rather than originality. When we come to things which are not obvious, and where finding an original line of thought is difficult, then we should consider originality in addition to presentation.

PHAEDRUS: I agree. What you say seems perfectly fair. So what I'll do is this. I'll grant that the man who is in love is in a worse state than the man who isn't. You can take that as read. But as for the rest of the speech, you must make it fuller and more convincing than Lysias', if you want to stand in beaten metal beside the Cypselids' offering at Olympia.

SOCRATES: I was only teasing you, Phaedrus, when I attacked your darling Lysias. Did you take me seriously? And do you really think I am going to try and rival his cleverness with something new, something more subtle?

PHAEDRUS: As for that, my friend, I have you

c   in the same hold you had me in. You have no choice but to speak as best you can. Otherwise we shall be driven to the banal repartee of the comedians. I warn you, don't go out of your way to make me quote your own words back at you: 'Socrates, if I don't know my Socrates, I have lost all memory of myself as well.' Or 'He wanted to speak, but then he went all coy.' You'd better face the fact that we're not leaving here until you tell me what it was you said your heart was full of. Here we are in a deserted

d   place, just the two of us. I'm younger than you, and stronger. For all these reasons, you must 'give ear unto my words'. Speak of your own accord. Don't choose to speak under duress.

SOCRATES: Seriously, Phaedrus, I'm an amateur. I shall make a fool of myself if I try to make an improvised speech, on the same subject, in competition with a professional speech-writer.

PHAEDRUS: Listen to this, and stop playing hard to get. I have something to say which will more or less compel you to speak.

SOCRATES: In that case, don't say it.

PHAEDRUS: No, I will say it. I shall make it an oath. I swear to you – but by whom? By which god?

e   Will this plane tree do? I hereby swear, that if you do not make your speech, right here by this same plane tree, I shall never show you, or tell you about, any speech, by anyone else, ever again.

SOCRATES: You've done it, you wretch. You've found the way to make me do what you want. I can't resist speeches.

PHAEDRUS: Then why do you keep trying to wriggle out of it?

SOCRATES: I'll stop, now you've taken that oath. I can never say 'no' to a treat of that sort.

PHAEDRUS: Very well. Speak.

SOCRATES: Shall I tell you what I'll do?

PHAEDRUS: What you'll do?

SOCRATES: I'll speak with my head covered. That'll be the quickest way of getting through my speech. Otherwise, if I look at you, I shall dry up in embarrassment.

PHAEDRUS: Just make your speech. That apart, you can do as you please.

SOCRATES: Come, ye Muses, you who are called clear-voiced – either from the nature of your song, or else from that musical nation, the Ligurians. 'Take up with me' the story which this fine gentleman is forcing me to relate. He already thinks his friend a wise man. May he now think him even wiser.   b

There was once a boy – well, almost a young man, really – and he was very beautiful. He had a vast number of lovers, one of whom was smart enough to have convinced the boy he was not in love with him, though actually he was, just as much as the others. One day he was pressing his claim, and trying to persuade the boy, just like Lysias, that he should grant his favours to the man who was not in love with him, rather than to the man who was. This is what he said.

'It is a universal rule, my boy, that if you want to make a right decision, there is only one place to   c start. You need to know what the decision is about; otherwise you are bound to miss out completely. Most people don't realize their ignorance of what each thing really is. They assume they do know, and so they do not agree on this at the outset of the enquiry. As they go on, they pay the predictable penalty – they contradict both themselves and each other. Let us not, you and I, allow the same thing to happen to us, now that we have identified it as a fault in others. The question at issue, for you and me, is whether you should embark upon a friendship with one who loves you, or one who doesn't.

d   So we must lay down an agreed definition of love – what its nature is, and what power it has. Then we can consult this definition, and refer to it in the course of our enquiry into its advantages and disadvantages.

'Well, that love is some form of desire is clear to anyone. And we also know that even when they are not in love, men desire what is beautiful. By what yardstick, then, can we tell the man who is in love from the man who is not? The next point to note is that for each of us there are two kinds of thing which rule and guide us; we follow them wherever they lead. One is our innate desire for pleasures, the other is acquired – a capacity for judgement, an aspiration towards what is best. Sometimes these two things in us are in agreement, but there are

e   times also when they are at odds with one another. First one, then the other, has the upper hand. When judgement is dominant, and directs us by rational argument towards what is best, we call this dominance "self-control". Desire, on the other hand, is

238   irrational. When it seizes power in us, and drags us towards pleasure, the name we give this power is excess.

'But then excess has many names, since it has many limbs and many forms. And whichever of these forms actually manifests itself on any occasion gives the person possessing it its own particular name – an ugly name, and one he would be better off without. If it is a question of food, then when desire overpowers both rational calculation of what is best and the other desires, it is called gluttony, and it will give the person possessing it b this same name. If it is a question of drink, on the other hand, and desire seizes the mastery, taking its owner in that direction, then it's plain what label he will have earned. As for all the other related names, of related desires, it is no less plain that he is called, as appropriate, by the name of the desire which has the mastery over him at any particular moment. And when it comes to the desire which is the subject of everything we have said so far, well, it should be pretty apparent by now, but I suppose what is explicit is always clearer than what is implicit. The irrational desire which gains the upper hand over the judgement which guides men towards what is right, has as its motive force the enjoyment of beauty. What is c more, it is strongly empowered in its drive towards physical beauty by the desires which are related to it. Winning the victory as it goes, it takes its name from this same power. It is called the power of love.'

Now, my dear Phaedrus, does it strike you, as it strikes me, that something supernatural has happened to me?

PHAEDRUS: It certainly has, Socrates. You

have been seized by a quite uncharacteristic talkativeness.

SOCRATES: Quiet, then, and listen to me. There really does seem to be something supernatural about this place. Don't be surprised if I am nymph-possessed at times as my speech progresses. Even now my utterance is bordering on the dithyrambic.

PHAEDRUS: Absolutely true.

SOCRATES: For that we have you to thank. But hear what follows; the danger may yet be averted, after all. Anyway, we can let god take care of that. Our job is to approach the boy again with our speech.

'Courage, then, my friend. It has now been laid down and defined what the subject of our enquiry actually is. That is our point of reference for the rest of our discussion, and the question is: what good or harm is the one who grants his favours likely to receive from the man in love or the man not in love? The man who is subject to desire, who is pleasure's slave, is presumably bound to be forever making the one he loves as pleasing to himself as he can. To a man who is sick anything is pleasing which offers no resistance; what is stronger, or equal, is objectionable. So a lover will not readily tolerate his boyfriend being stronger, or becoming his equal. He spends his whole time trying to make him weaker and inferior. Now, ignorant is weaker than wise, cowardly than brave, inarticulate than persuasive, slow than quick-witted. If a lover finds these kinds of faults, and others besides, either making their appearance in the mind of the one he loves, or already there by nature, he is bound to be delighted by them, and encourage further faults, or else lose his immediate pleasure. He is bound to be jealous, and by keeping him from good company of the kind which would most help the boy to become a man, he will do him great harm. But the greatest harm will be to keep him from the thing which would most help him gain in wisdom. This is, of course, divine philosophy. A lover is bound to keep his boyfriend well away from it, fearing the contempt it would arouse. And in general, he is bound so to engineer things that the boy remains completely ignorant, and looks to his lover for everything; that way he gives most satisfaction to the lover, and does most harm to himself. So as far as understanding goes, a man in love is no useful guide or companion.

'The next thing we must look at is the body — its physical condition and training. What sort of physical condition, and what manner of training, will the man who is under compulsion to follow pleasure rather than goodness choose for the person under his control? We shall find him pursuing one who is soft, not hard, one brought up in dappled shade rather than full sun, a stranger to man's work and the sweat of labour, familiar only with a life which is sheltered and unmanly, one who makes himself attractive with borrowed colours and charms, for want of any of his own, and adopts all the other behaviour which goes with this. We know all about this behaviour. It is not worth spending any more time on. I'll put the whole thing in a nutshell, and then move on. In time of war or other emergency, a physique of this

kind encourages the enemy, and makes friends and
even lovers anxious.

'That's so obvious that we can take it for
granted, and deal with the next point. What use or
e   harm will the friendship and advice of the lover
be to us when it comes to possessions? No one
can be in any doubt – least of all the lover – that
his dearest wish is for the one he loves to lose the
closest, most loyal and most divine possessions he
has. He would be happy for him to lose father
and mother, relatives and friends, since he regards
them as people who will obstruct and condemn
240   that association which brings him most pleasure.
What is more, if the boy has property, in the form
of money or possessions of any other kind, he
won't regard him as such an easy catch, nor so
manageable once caught. This makes it an absolute
certainty that the lover will resent his boyfriend's
possession of property, and be pleased when it is
lost. And further, in his desire to enjoy the sweet
fruits of his own pleasure for the longest time
possible, a lover would wish upon his boyfriend a
life that was unmarried, childless and homeless for
the longest time possible.

'Many are life's evils, but with most of them some
b   divine power or spirit has added a momentary mixture of pleasure. A flatterer, for example, is a fear-
some creature and a great menace. Yet nature has
given the flatterer a touch of charm as well, which
is not wholly unpleasing. Or a courtesan, you might
say, is a bad lot – as are many other similar creatures
and their ways. Yet on a day-to-day basis they have
the property of being excellent company. For a

boyfriend, on the other hand, not only is the lover
a bad influence; he is also, of all people to spend
time with, the worst company. There's an old saying: "Crabbed age and youth cannot live together."   c
I imagine similarity in age leads to similar pleasures,
and then converts similarity into friendship. Yet
even people of the same age can have enough of
one another.

'And that's not all. Compulsion, for anybody, in
any situation, is regarded as a burden. And compulsion is unmistakably what the lover brings to bear
upon his boyfriend, in addition to the dissimilarity
between them. It is an older man keeping company
with a younger, refusing to leave him alone, day
or night. He is driven by a frenzied compulsion,   d
which goads him on by continually offering him
the pleasure of seeing the one he loves, hearing
him, touching him, experiencing him with every
sense. It is a pleasure to be in close attendance on
him. But what about the one he loves? What kind
of compensation or enjoyment does the lover give
him, to prevent his reaching a state of utter dis-
gust? After all, he has to spend as much time with
his lover as his lover spends with him. He sees the
face of age, its youthful freshness gone, with all
that that implies. Even a description of it is pretty
distasteful, let alone the constant additional   e
demand that he should deal with the real thing. He
finds himself a prisoner, jealously guarded, all the
time and in all his contacts. He has to listen to
extravagant and inappropriate praise, and likewise
blame — intolerable when the lover is sober, but
when he is drunk, and really lets himself go,

speaking freely and without pause, then it is more than intolerable, it is humiliating.

'While he remains in love, this is all pernicious and distasteful. When he stops being in love, then he cannot be relied upon in that future for which he promised so much, with so many oaths and entreaties. He managed, with some difficulty, to get the boy to put up with the tedium of his company in the past, in the hope of good things to come. But when the time comes for him to redeem his promises, he changes to a new lord and master within himself. Reason and good sense take the place of passion and madness, and he becomes a different person, though his boyfriend does not realize it. He asks the lover to repay past favours, reminding him of his actions and words, in the belief that he is still talking to the same person. The lover is embarrassed. He cannot bring himself to say that he is now somebody else; that he cannot make good the oaths and promises of the irrational power which drove him before, since he has now recovered his reason and regained his senses; that he does not want, by behaving as he behaved then, to become like that man – in fact, *become* that man – again.

'As a result of this he takes to his heels, yesterday's lover. He is compelled to default. The coin comes down tails instead of heads, and now it is his turn to run away as fast as he can. As the boy is forced to become the pursuer, he grows angry, and calls upon the gods. What he has failed to realize, right from the start, is that it was a mistake ever to grant his favours to a man who was in love, and therefore not in his right mind. Much better to have granted them to the man who was not in love, who did have his wits about him. Otherwise he would necessarily be giving himself to one who is unreliable, bad-tempered, jealous, disagreeable, a threat to his property, a threat to his physical fitness, but above all a threat to the development of his soul – than which, in truth, in the eyes of men and gods alike, there neither is nor ever will be anything of greater value.

'Well, my boy, those are the things you should be thinking about. You have to realize that a lover's friendship is without goodwill. You are like food to him when he is hungry. As wolf loves lamb, so lover loves his boy.'

There you are, Phaedrus, as advertised. It's all you're going to get from me, so can we please let the speech end there.

PHAEDRUS: Oh, I thought that was just the first half. I thought you'd have as much again to say about the man who is not in love, the reasons for granting favours to him rather than the lover, and all the advantages he has. Instead of which, you've stopped, Socrates. Why?

SOCRATES: For heaven's sake, Phaedrus. I'm long past dithyramb already, and well into epic by now. Or hadn't you noticed? And that was just during the critical part. If I start praising the other man, what do you think I shall do then? You realize, don't you, that I shall be visibly inspired by the Nymphs, to whom you made a point of introducing me. So I'll just say, in summary, that for every fault we have found on one side, there is a corresponding virtue present on the other. There's no need to say more than that, because that satisfactorily defines both. So my account can now meet the fate it deserves, while I cross the river here, and make my escape before you can force me into anything more ambitious.

PHAEDRUS: Not yet, Socrates. Wait till the heat of the day passes. Look, it's just about midday – what's known as the 'point of no return'. Why don't we stay, discuss what's been said so far, and then go when it gets cooler.

SOCRATES: Phaedrus, you're a marvel. There's no other word for it. Your passion for speeches is out of this world. If you ask me, you're the greatest originator of speeches living – either making them yourself, or in one way or another forcing others to make them. I don't count Simmias the Theban, but apart from him, you come first. And now you've done it again, I think. You're the cause of my making another speech.

PHAEDRUS: I shan't quarrel with that. But how? What sort of speech?

SOCRATES: I was just going to cross the river, my friend, when I had that strange spiritual experience, that sign I sometimes have – the one which always tells me not to do what I'm just on the point of doing. And I thought I heard a voice from this very spot, forbidding me to leave without purifying myself, now that I have offended against religion. I must be a bit of a seer, though not much of one. More like someone who is barely literate – just enough for my own needs. So I have a pretty good idea what I have done wrong. Believe me, my friend, the soul is a little bit prophetic too. There has been something bothering me for a while now, even when I was making my speech. I was worried that, in Ibycus' words, I might

> by some offence   d
> Against the gods win great renown from men.

Now I can see what my offence was.

PHAEDRUS: What was it?

SOCRATES: It was horrible, Phaedrus, horrible, that speech you brought with you, and the one you forced me to make.

PHAEDRUS: In what way?

SOCRATES: It was stupid, and to some extent blasphemous. Can a speech be more horrible than that?

PHAEDRUS: No, it can't – if you're right about it being blasphemous.

SOCRATES: Well, don't you believe Eros to be the son of Aphrodite, and therefore a god?

PHAEDRUS: He is said to be.

SOCRATES: Not by Lysias he isn't. Nor by your speech. I call it yours, though it was spoken by me,   e under your spell. If Eros is a god or spirit of some kind – as in fact he certainly is – he cannot be something evil. Yet both the speeches we have just made spoke of him as if he were. So in that respect at least they offended against Eros. Beyond that there was their prize stupidity. They had nothing true or healthy to say, yet they solemnly pretended   243 to be of some importance, in the hope of deceiving a few poor specimens of humanity somewhere, and gaining their approval. I don't know about you, my friend, but I feel a compelling need to purify myself.

There is a traditional form of purification for those who do wrong in the telling of stories. Homer didn't know about it, though Stesichorus did. He lost his sight because of the harsh things he said about Helen. But he didn't claim to be ignorant of the cause of his blindness, as Homer did. Knowing his art, he understood the reason, and quickly wrote these lines:

> I told a tale untrue. You made no voyage
> In fine decked ships, nor came to Troy's high tower.

As soon as he'd completed his 'Palinode', as it is called, he at once regained his sight. I am going to be, in one respect at least, wiser than the poets were. I am going to try and make my palinode *before* anything happens to me as a result of the evil things I have said about Eros. I shall speak bareheaded. No need to cover my head in shame, as I did before.

PHAEDRUS: Socrates, that's the best possible news you could have given me.

SOCRATES: The reason for that, Phaedrus, is that you're aware of the immorality of our two speeches – both the one I made and the one you read from the book. Imagine someone listening to us: some fine, generous character who was in love, or perhaps had been in love in the past, with someone like himself. When he heard us saying that lovers pick tremendous quarrels on trivial pretexts, and that they feel jealous and vindictive towards their boyfriends, don't you think he'd be bound to imagine we'd been brought up on the waterfront somewhere, that we'd never seen a love which is free, between equals? He wouldn't dream of accepting our criticisms of Eros.   d

PHAEDRUS: Very probably not, Socrates.

SOCRATES: When I think of this man, then I for one am ashamed. And I fear Eros himself. I want to wash away, as it were, the bitter taste of what we've heard with a clean, fresh draught. And that would be my advice to Lysias too – to write another speech as soon as he can. Let him tell the boy that he should grant his favours, on a free and equal basis, to the man who *is* in love with him rather than the man who is not.

PHAEDRUS: That's what will happen, rest assured. If you make your speech in praise of the lover, Lysias will have no choice. He will be compelled by me to respond with a speech on the same   e theme.

SOCRATES: I don't doubt it for a moment, you being the person you are.

PHAEDRUS: Don't worry about that, then. Make your speech.

SOCRATES: Where is the boy I was talking to earlier? He ought to hear this part too. If he goes off without hearing it, he may grant his favours to the man who is not in love before anyone can stop him.

PHAEDRUS: Here he is. Right beside you all along – any time you want him.

SOCRATES: Very well.

Now, the first thing to be clear about, my good-looking boy, is this. That first speech was really the work of Phaedrus the son of Pythocles, from the   244 deme of Myrrhinous. The speech I am going to

make now is the work of Stesichorus the son of
Euphemus, from Himera. What it must say is this:
there is no truth in the idea that if you have a lover,
you should still grant your favours to the man who
is not in love with you, because he is sane, while the
lover is mad. If it were that simple – if madness
were always an evil – it would be a good idea. But
it isn't that simple. We owe the greatest of blessings
to madness, provided it comes as a gift from the
gods. In their madness the prophetess at Delphi,
b   and the priestesses at Dodona, do much that is good
for Greece – both for individuals and states. When
sane, they do little or nothing. And then there's the
Sibyl and others, who with their inspired gift of
prophecy have made many predictions for many
people, and given them good guidance for the
future. If we are going to talk about them, we could
go on for a long time without saying anything which
isn't well known to everyone already.

However, there is one piece of evidence worth
mentioning. Among the ancients, those who gave
things their names did not see madness as something shameful, or as a term of reproach. Otherwise
they wouldn't have attached this name, 'manic', to
c   the fairest of the arts – the art of discerning the
future. No, they gave it this name as a mark of
approval, when the madness comes as a divine gift.
In their ignorance, people nowadays have added a
't' to it, making it 'mantic'. It's the same with the
study of the future made by people who are not
insane – using the flight of birds and other portents.
Long ago people gave it the name 'oionoïstic', a
word which reflects the rational application of

intelligence and inquiry to human thinking. These
days people call it 'oiônistic', giving it a long 'o' to   d
make it sound more important. Now, to whatever
extent the mantic art – name for name, and power
for power – is something more complete and of
greater value than the oionistic, to that extent past
ages bear witness that madness sent by god is a finer
thing than human sanity.

Then again, there are those great afflictions and
hardships suffered by some families, arising perhaps
from some long-standing guilt. Madness appears
where it must, with prophetic power, and finds a
way out, taking refuge in prayers to the gods and   e
divine services. Finding in these its rites of purification, it puts its possessor out of danger, both
for the present and for the future, discovering a
release from his present troubles for him who is
maddened and possessed in the right way.

A third form of possession and madness comes   245
from the Muses. Taking hold of a soft, virgin soul,
it rouses it to a state of poetic ecstasy, in lyric or
some other form, and so educates later ages by
celebrating countless deeds of days gone by. But as
for the man who arrives at poetry's door without
the Muses' madness, in the belief that technical skill
will make him a good poet, he remains incomplete,
himself and his works, and disappears before the
poetry of madness.

All these and more I can tell you about – the   b
achievements of madness when it comes from the
gods. So that's one thing we can set our minds at
rest about. Nor need we be troubled by any scare-
mongering argument suggesting that we should

choose the sane man as a friend in preference to the disturbed. We should award the prize to such an argument only if it can demonstrate something else as well – that the love the gods send is not of benefit to lover and loved alike. Our job is to prove the opposite, that it is our great good fortune that

c madness of this kind is given to us by the gods. The proof will not convince those who are too clever, but it will convince those who are wise.

The first thing to do, then, is look at the behaviour and actions of soul – divine and human – in order to understand the truth about its nature. Our proof begins like this:

All soul is immortal. That is because what is always in motion is immortal, whereas that which moves something else, and is moved by something else, ceases to live when it ceases to move. Only what is self-moving never ceases to move, since it never gets away from itself. Moreover it is the source and first principle of motion in the other things which move. A first principle is without a

d beginning. Everything which comes into existence must necessarily come into existence from a first principle, but a first principle itself cannot come into existence from anything. If a first principle *could* come into existence from something, it would no longer be a first principle. Since it has no beginning, it must necessarily be indestructible as well, since if a first principle perishes, then neither will it come into being from anything else, nor will anything else come into being from it, given that everything has to come into being from a first principle.

In this way, then, that which moves itself is the

first principle of motion. It is not possible for it either to be destroyed or to come into being. Other-wise the whole universe and everything which comes to be would collapse upon itself and come to an end, having no new source of motion to bring it back into being. And since what is self-moving has been shown to be immortal, we can claim, with a clear conscience, that this is the essence and defining characteristic of soul. Any body whose motion comes from outside itself is without soul; if its motion is within itself – from itself – it does have soul, this being the nature of soul. If this is so, if that which moves itself is nothing other than soul, soul must necessarily be without beginning and immortal.

Very well. On the subject of its immortality, that is enough. But something should now be said about its form. To tell you what sort of thing it really is would call for a lengthy explanation – one altogether and in every way beyond human power. To tell you what it is *like*, on the other hand, is within human capability, and briefer. So let us approach it in that way. Let us liken it to a winged charioteer and his team, viewed all together as a single moving body. For the gods, the horses and charioteers are all good themselves, and of good pedigree; for everyone else, there is a mixture. In the first place, our driver has a pair of horses under the reins. Sec-ondly, one of his horses is handsome and noble, and its pedigree the same, while the other is the opposite, and of opposite pedigree. So for us, driv-ing is bound to be difficult and unpleasant. How it comes about, then, that a living creature is called

e

246

b

both mortal and immortal, we must now try to explain.

All soul has charge of what is without soul. It traverses the entire universe, coming to be in different shapes at different times. In its perfect, winged state it moves above the earth; its domain is the whole cosmos. But the soul that has lost its wings is carried along until it can take hold of something solid. There it settles, and occupies an earthy body. This body appears to be self-moving, because of the soul's power; and the whole thing, soul and body joined together, is called a living creature, and acquires the name 'mortal'. As for calling it immortal, that comes from no reasoned argument at all. Because we have never seen or adequately conceived a god, we picture an immortal creature of some sort, possessed of soul, possessed of body, and with the two combined for the whole of time. Anyway, let all this, and our account of it, be as god will have it. Now it is for us to understand the reason why wings are lost, why they fall away from a soul. It is more or less like this.

The natural property of a wing is to lift what is heavy, raising it on high, where the race of the gods lives. Of all the things to do with the body, it has the greatest share in the divine; and the divine is beautiful, wise, good, and everything of that kind. This is what the soul's plumage mostly feeds on, what makes it grow; whereas what is ugly and bad – all the opposites – causes it to waste away and perish. First and foremost in heaven is Zeus, driving a winged chariot. He travels ahead of the others, taking thought for all things, and setting all things in order. A host of gods and spirits follows him, arranged in eleven companies. This is because Hestia remains by herself in the house of the gods. Among the rest, those who have a place allocated in the number of the twelve take the lead, as ruler gods, in the positions assigned to each.

247

Within the heavens are many blessed sights, on the paths round which the happy race of gods make their way, each of them carrying out his own task. They are followed by whoever, at any particular time, has the inclination and ability to do so; there is no place, in the dance of the gods, for envy. When they go to their feasting and banqueting, they climb up to the topmost vault of heaven. There the ascent is steep. The gods' chariots are balanced and manageable; they travel with ease. For the rest it is difficult, since the horse with an element of evil in its nature drags them down. If any of the charioteers has an ill-trained horse, it weighs him down, and pulls him back to earth, where the soul is confronted by extremes of hardship and suffering. The souls which we call immortal, when they reach the summit, make their way to the outside, and stand upon the back of the heavens; standing there, they are carried round by the rotation, and behold the things outside the heavens.

b

c

This place which lies beyond heaven has never yet been praised by any poet here on earth, nor will any poet ever do justice to it. But I will tell you. After all, one must have the courage to speak the truth, especially if one is speaking *about* the truth. Being which really and truly is — without colour, without form, intangible, visible to reason alone, the helmsman of the soul, the being to which the category of true knowledge applies – dwells in this place. Since the mind of a god, as of any soul which cares to accept what is right for it, is fed on intellect and pure knowledge, it rejoices when it finally sees what really is. Beholding the truth, it thrives, it draws sustenance from it, until finally the rotation brings it round in a circle, back to the same place. In this journey round it sees justice itself; it sees self-control; it sees knowledge – not knowledge combined with coming-to-be, not the knowledge which varies, I take it, in the varied objects which we now describe as being, but that which truly is knowledge because it is in what truly is. It feasts its eyes, similarly, on the other things which truly are, then sinks back to the inside of heaven, and returns home. When it gets there, the charioteer stands the horses at their manger. He puts ambrosia before them, and with it nectar to drink.

Such is the life of the gods. As for the others, the one which follows a god, and has grown most like him, lifts the head of its charioteer into the world outside, and is taken round by the rotation. But it has trouble with its horses, and can barely glimpse the things which really are. Another is now above and now below; its horses fight against it, and it sees some things, but not others. The rest follow, all struggling upwards, but unable to make it; they are borne round below the surface, trampling and jostling one another as one tries to get ahead of the other. The result is confusion, conflict and violent exertion, in which many are lamed, through the failings of their charioteers, and many,

many are those whose wings are broken. All these suffer great hardship; they fail in their attempt, and depart without seeing what really is. And once departed, they feed on what they imagine nourishes them. Why are they so eager to see the 'plain of truth' in the place where it is? Because the pastur- age which is right for the best part of the soul is in fact to be found in the meadow there, and because this is what the wing which lifts the soul   c naturally feeds on.

Hear then Necessity's decree: any soul which follows in the train of a god, and catches some glimpse of what is true, remains free from suffering until its next time round. If it always succeeds in doing this, then it always remains unharmed. But sometimes it is unable to keep up, and cannot see; through some mischance it is filled with forget- fulness and weakness, and is weighed down; and being weighed down, it loses its wings and falls to earth. If this happens, then the law is not to implant it, on its first time of being born, in some wild   d beast. No, the soul which has seen most will enter into a seed from which will come a man who is destined to be a lover of wisdom or lover of beauty, a follower of the Muses or Eros; the next soul in a lawful monarch, or a born general or leader; the third in a statesman, or perhaps some head of a household or businessman; the fourth in a trainer of athletes, a lover of physical exercise, or someone marked out for the healing of the body; the fifth will have the life of a seer or leader of a cult; the sixth will be suited by the life of somebody engaged   e in the imitative arts, a poet perhaps; the seventh by the life of a craftsman or farmer; the eighth by that of a sophist or crowd-pleaser; the ninth by that of a tyrant.

In all these lives, the man who lives justly gets a better deal, the man who lives unjustly a worse deal. It is ten thousand years before each soul returns to the place from which it has come. That is how long it takes for its wings to grow – except for the one who follows wisdom without self-seeking, or who has loved a young boy in a philosophical way. As the third millennium comes round these souls, if they have chosen this life three times running, grow wings and so depart, in the three thousandth year. The rest, at the end of that first life, come up for judgment. And when they have been judged, some go to the places of punishment beneath the earth, and pay the penalty in full, while others are borne aloft, by Justice, to some place in the heavens, where they spend their time in the manner they have earned by the lives they lived in human form. In the thousandth year each class turns up for the allocation and selection of their second life; each chooses the life it wants. At that point a human soul can enter into the life of an animal, and anyone who was once a human can go back to being human from being an animal.

The soul which has never seen the truth will never take this human shape, because a human being must be able to grasp generalizations arising out of a number of individual perceptions, and shaped into a single judgement by the power of reason. This is a recollection of the things our soul saw once, when it was travelling with a god, looking

249

b

c

down on the things we now describe as being, and lifting up its head towards what truly is. That is why it is right that only the mind of the philosopher has wings. In his memory, to the best of his ability, he is always close to those things whose closeness makes gods godlike. Only the man who makes good use of memories of this kind, and is fully initiated in perfect rites, can become truly perfect. Withdrawing from human interests, and coming close to   d
what is divine, he is criticized by the many; they say he is out of his mind. They do not realize, the many, that he is possessed by god.

This, then, is my description of the fourth kind of madness. Now I'll tell you my conclusion. When a man sees beauty here, in this life, he is reminded of true beauty. He grows wings, and stands there fluttering them, eager to fly upwards, but unable to do so. Yet still he looks upwards, as birds do, and takes no notice of what is below; and so he is accused of being mad. My conclusion is quite different. Of all forms of divine possession, this is   c
the best – and has the best origins – both for him who has it and for him who shares in it. It is this madness which the lover of beauty must experience if he is to be called a lover. To repeat, it is the nature of every human soul that it has seen the things that are; otherwise it could not have become the human thing it is. But the task of recollecting what it saw   250
there from what it now sees here is not an easy one for every soul, either for the ones which caught only a quick glimpse of what was up there, or for those which fell to earth and fared badly down here, being led into injustice by bad company of one sort or

another, and so forgetting the holy things they saw up there.

There remain a few souls whose recollection is adequate. These, when they see some likeness of what is there, are dumbfounded; they are no longer masters of themselves, though their perception is unclear, and so they do not realize what is happening to them. In the day-to-day likenesses of justice and self-control, and the other things which are valuable to souls, there is little power to illumine; nevertheless, weak as our organs of perception are, it is possible – though hard, and few achieve it – to approach these images, and detect the nature of the thing they are images of. Before, its beauty was plain to see, when they joined in the joyful dance, and saw that blessed sight and spectacle – we ourselves following with Zeus, others with some other of the gods. Then they were initiated into what we should rightly call the most blessed of the mysteries. Celebrating those rites, whole in ourselves and with no experience of the evil which lay in wait for us, we were initiated, and granted the final revelation, in the pure light of day, of those manifestations which are whole, uncompounded, unmoving and full of joy. Ourselves pure, we were not entombed in this thing we now call our body, imprisoned in it like oysters as we carry it round with us.

Let this be our tribute paid to memory. It has led me, out of nostalgia for what I saw then, to speak now at considerable length. As for beauty, it shone forth, as we said, in that company; and now that we have entered upon our life here, we find it sparkling most brilliantly, through the medium of the most brilliant of our senses. The sharpest of our physical senses is sight. It cannot help us to see wisdom — that would arouse an awesome love indeed, if it allowed so brilliant a likeness of itself to come before our eyes. The same goes for whatever else arouses love, leaving only beauty with the property of being wholly visible and wholly able to inspire love.

Now, the man who is not recently initiated, or who has become corrupted, does not move eagerly from what he sees here, beauty's namesake, to the real beauty he saw there. He does not gaze at it and worship it. No, he gives himself up to pleasure, going at it like a four-footed animal, and trying to father offspring. Excess is his companion, and he follows pleasure without fear or embarrassment, in defiance of nature. What happens to the man who is recently initiated, the one who saw much of what was shown him, is quite different. When he sees a good likeness of beauty — a face or bodily shape like those of a god — the first thing he does is shiver feverishly, and there comes over him something of the awe he felt before. Then, gazing at it, he worships the beauty he sees, as he would a god; only the fear of being thought completely mad stops him sacrificing to his boyfriend as to the statue of a god. When he sees him, a change comes over him — the sweating and high temperature you would expect after the shivering. His temperature rises with the stream of beauty coming to him through his eyes, and his wings grow, like a plant watered by this stream. The area round the shoot, which in the past has locked solid, preventing any growth, is thawed by the rise in temperature. As the nourishment pours in, the quills of the feathers expand, and they start sprouting from their roots all over the soul, below the surface; for the entire soul was once winged. Meanwhile the soul becomes inflamed, and throbs all over.

It's the same with cutting teeth. When teeth start growing, there is a tingling and itching in the gums, and that is what the soul of the man who is starting to grow wings feels like. It becomes inflamed, it itches and tickles, as it starts growing its wings. Sometimes, then, it looks at the boy's beauty, and receives the particles of it which come flooding in – hence 'waves' of desire. Then it is watered and thawed; it finds relief from its pain, and is filled with joy. At other times it is cut off, and becomes parched. Then the openings the feathers sprout from dry up completely; they close, cutting off the growth of the feather, which is trapped inside along with the desire, throbbing like a pulse. Each feather pushes against its own opening, so that the entire soul stings all over, maddened by the pain. Yet still it delights in the recollection of the beauty it has seen.

Subject to these conflicting impulses, it is bewildered by the unfamiliarity of its feelings. Unsure what to do, it is driven into a frenzy, and in its madness it cannot sleep at night, nor by day remain where it is; full of desire, it rushes to the place where it thinks it will see the one who has this beauty. And when it does see him, it lets desire flow in like an irrigating flood, freeing the pores which were obstructed. Finding relief from the stinging

and the birth-pangs, it once again for a time enjoys
this sweetest of pleasures. It does not readily give it   252
up, regarding the beautiful one as more important
than anyone else. It forgets mother, brothers,
friends, the whole lot of them. As the man's wealth
is destroyed through neglect, it pays no regard. And
it now views with contempt the conventions and
proprieties on which it once prided itself. It is ready
to be a slave, and to sleep wherever it is allowed, so
long as it is close to its heart's desire. Besides the
awe it feels before the possessor of beauty, it has   b
also found the sole healer of its great suffering. This
is the feeling, my good-looking boy – you to whom
I am making my speech – which men call 'love'; if
I tell you what the gods call it, you are probably
young enough to laugh at me. Some of the Homeric
school, I believe, quote lines about Eros from the
lesser poems. One of the lines is a complete disgrace – it doesn't really scan at all. They go like this:

> To mortal men our thought'll then
>   Not come as a surprise:
> 'Eros, the winged one,' we say;
>   The gods say otherwise –
> It 'wingèd' is 'ptero-', not 'Eros' but 'Pteros'
>   The name that must arise.

This you can believe or not, as you choose. But   c
certainly the cause of people being in love, and what
it feels like when you are, are exactly as I have said.
    Any follower of Zeus who is caught by love can
endure the burden of the winged god with some
composure. Those who are servants of Ares, who
made their circuit of heaven with him, when they

are taken by love and think they are being wronged
by the one they love, become homicidal, quite prepared to offer up themselves and their boyfriends
in sacrifice. The same with all the other gods. Each
person serves and imitates, as best he can, the god
in whose train he originally followed. This is how
he lives, while he is uncorrupted and spending the
first of his lives here; and this is the manner of his
friendship and bearing both towards those he loves
and towards others. Each man selects, from among
the beautiful, a love to suit his character; he treats
him like a sacred image, working on him and embel-
lishing him as if this were his god in person. He
wants to honour him, and perform his rites. So
those who belong to Zeus look for someone whose
soul is like Zeus to be the object of their love. Is he
a lover of wisdom, they ask themselves? Is he a
natural leader? And when they find him and fall in
love with him, they do everything they can to help
him turn out like that.

   If they have not embarked on this activity before,
this is the point at which they start, finding instruction where they can, and also pursuing the enquiry
for themselves. And as they try to follow the trail
which leads to the discovery within themselves of
the nature of their own god, they succeed when
they are compelled to fix their gaze intently on the
god. Grasping him in recollection, and inspired by
him, they take their habits and behaviour from him,
to the fullest extent that a man can have a share in
a god. And because they regard the one they love
as the cause of all this, they love him still more. If
they draw their inspiration from the well of Zeus,

they pour it over the soul of the one they love, making him as much like their own god as possible. Equally, those who were followers of Hera look for someone kingly. And when they find him, they treat him in exactly the same way.

Those who were with Apollo – and each of the gods – follow the pattern of their god. They want their boy to be of this nature, and when they find a boyfriend who is, then imitating the god themselves, and persuading and educating the boy, they bring him, each one so far as lies in his power, into the way of life and likeness of the god. They show none of that jealousy or smallmindedness towards their boyfriend. Their actions are governed by the attempt to bring him into a full likeness, in every respect, to the best of their ability, of themselves and the god they serve. So the enthusiasm of true lovers, and its outcome – at least if they gain the object of their enthusiasm in the way I describe – is thus a fine thing, and the cause of happiness, coming as it does from the friend who is maddened by love to the one who is loved, if he is caught. And if he is caught, he is caught like this.

At the beginning of our story we divided every soul into three parts – two having the form of horses, the third that of a charioteer. Let that still remain our model. Of the horses, one is good, we say, the other not. We did not explain the goodness of the good horse, or the badness of the bad horse; we must describe them now. The one in the position of honour is upright in form, well-proportioned, with a high neck and hooked nose. It is white in appearance, with dark eyes. A lover of glory, but with restraint and modesty, the companion of true renown. It has never felt the whip, responding simply to the charioteer's word of command. The other is crooked, a great big jumble of parts put together any old how. Strong in the neck, short in the windpipe, with a flat nose, dark coat and grey bloodshot eyes, the companion of excess and boasting. Shaggy round the ears, deaf, slow to obey even whip and spur together.

When the charioteer first sees the face he loves, warming his whole soul with the sight, he begins to be filled with tickling and the pains of desire. The horse which obeys the charioteer is controlled, now as always, by modesty; it keeps itself in check, and does not leap upon the one it loves. But the other stops paying any attention at all to the charioteer's spur or whip; it starts violently forward, to the great confusion of its fellow and the charioteer. It drives them towards the boy, and forces them to bring up the question of sexual pleasure. At first the other horse and the charioteer resist, annoyed at the horrifying and unnatural thing they are being driven to. But in the end, seeing no end to the evil, they let themselves be carried along, giving in and agreeing to do what they are told. They come up close to him, and see the dazzling face of the boy they love. When the charioteer sees this, his recollection is carried back to the nature of beauty. Again he sees it, standing side by side with self-control, on a holy pedestal. The sight fills him with fear; he falls back, overcome with awe, and this makes him drag on the reins with such violence as to bring both horses back on their quarters. The good horse does not

pull, and comes readily, the rogue horse with great
reluctance. They draw back a little, the one in shame
and horror covering the entire soul in sweat, while
the other, once free of the pain of the bit and its fall,
barely recovers its breath before angrily blaming the
charioteer and its fellow. It heaps abuse on them
for their cowardly and unmanly desertion of their
post and their partnership. Again it tries to compel
them to make an advance, against their will, and   d
only grudgingly agrees when they ask to put it off
till another time.

When the appointed time comes, they both pretend they have forgotten. Plunging, neighing, and
pulling for his head, he reminds them, and forces
them to approach the boy once more with the same
suggestion. As soon as they come near, he sticks
his head down and his tail out, taking the bit
between his teeth, and pulling shamelessly. To the
charioteer, the same thing happens again – more   e
strongly than before. He recoils, as if from a
trap. More strongly than before, he wrests the bit
from the horse's teeth, bloodying the foul-mouthed
tongue and jaws, and bringing the horse down, legs
and haunches on the ground, in agony. The same
thing happens, over and over again, until the bad
horse gives up its demands. Humbled, it accepts
the charioteer's guidance. Now when it sees the
beautiful one, it dies of fright. And so it finally
comes about that the soul of the lover pursues the
boy in fear and reverence.

This is the lover who is not pretending, but who
genuinely feels this emotion. He worships the boy,   255
and will do anything for him. The boy is naturally

well-disposed, in any case, to someone who does things for him, even though he may once have been prejudiced against him by things he heard from his schoolfellows or anyone else. They may have said it was wrong to have anything to do with a lover, and this may have led the boy to reject him. But now, as time passes, his age and needs lead him to admit the lover to his company, since fate ordains

b that evil shall never be friend to evil, and that good shall never not be friend to good. So he allows the lover's advances, and accepts his company and conversation; and as he comes close, the altruism of the lover overwhelms the one who is loved. He realizes that, compared with this inspired friend, the entire company of his other friends and relatives has nothing to offer in the way of friendship. If he continues like this, he meets his lover – and that includes touching him – in the gymnasium and at other social events. Then the springs of that stream,

c to which Zeus, when he was in love with Ganymede, gave the name desire, flow freely over the lover, partly sinking into him and partly spilling over as he overflows.

As a breeze or echo rebounds from smooth hard surfaces, and returns in the direction from which it came, so the stream of beauty flows back to the beautiful one through his eyes, which are the normal pathway to the soul. Arriving there, it sets his

d heart fluttering, then moistens the passages of the feathers, making the wings grow, and filling the soul of the one who is loved in its turn with love. He loves, yes, but what he loves he cannot say. He does not know, and cannot describe, what has happened to him. It is as if he had picked up an eye complaint from someone, without being able to put a name to it. He does not realize that what he sees in his lover, as in a looking-glass, is himself. When the lover is there, then like the lover he finds release from his pain. When he is not there, then, again like the lover, he misses him and is missed. His return of love is a reflection of love, though he calls it — for so he thinks of it — affection rather than love. His desire is similar to the lover's, but weaker: the desire to see, to touch, to kiss, to go to bed with him.

And sure enough, as you would expect, this is the next step. So when they are in bed together, the lover's ill-disciplined horse has a suggestion to make to its charioteer; it thinks it deserves a small reward after all its sacrifices. The boy's horse has nothing to say; swelling with confused desire, he embraces the lover and kisses him, welcoming him as a true friend. And when they go to bed together, this horse is prepared, for its part, to say 'yes' to the lover, should he ask for sexual satisfaction. Its yoke-fellow, on the other hand, supported by the charioteer, opposes the suggestion with modesty and rational argument. If their better natures win the day, and guide them towards the disciplined life of philosophy, then the life they live here is blessed and harmonious. They are masters of themselves, and decorous in their behaviour; they have enslaved that which encourages the growth of evil in the soul, and set free what encourages the growth of excellence. On their death they grow wings and become weightless, having won the first of the three

e

256

b

falls in these, the true Olympics. Greater good than this can neither human virtue nor divine inspiration offer a man.

If they adopt a lower way of life – unphilosophical, yet not without ambition – then I suppose, when they have been drinking, or in some other moment of weakness, the two undisciplined horses may catch them both off their guard, and bring the two of them togther. Then they may make that choice which is generally called the most blessed, and act on it. And once they have acted on it, they continue with it from then on – but not too often, since their mind only half approves of what they are doing. This pair also are friends to one another, though less so than the other pair, both during the time of physical passion and when passion is spent. And so they spend their lives, in the belief that they have given and received the most powerful assurances, which it would be wrong ever to break by becoming enemies. On their deaths, on their departure from the body, they do not have wings, but they have made the first move towards growing them. So the madness of lovers brings them no small reward, since the rule is that anyone who has started on the journey beneath the heavens should not go into the darkness, to the journey beneath the earth. They are to be happy, spending their lives in the light and travelling with one another. Together they grow wings – when they do – like for like, as a reward for their love.

These are the great gifts, my child, the divine gifts, which the friendship of a lover will bring you. From the one who is not a lover you will get a mixture of familiarity and human prudence, doling out human benefits piecemeal, and producing, in the soul of his dear one, a worldliness which is praised as a virtue by most people, but which will cause him to roll mindlessly round the earth, and under the earth, for nine millennia.

257

That, sweet Eros, is my palinode offered to you in payment – the fairest and finest in my power, seeing that it was compelled, on Phaedrus' account, to use language that was somewhat poetical. I ask your pardon for my earlier speech, and your blessing on this one. Look kindly on me. Be gentle with me. Do not be angry, and take away or damage the skill you gave me in matters of love. May I be respected, more even than now, by those who are beautiful. As for our previous speech, if Phaedrus and I said anything you found offensive, you must blame Lysias, the father of our speech. Stop allowing him to make speeches of that kind, and point him in the direction of philosophy, like his brother Polemarchus. Then his lover here can stop trying to have it both ways, as he is now, and devote his life to a love where the speeches are all in the pursuit of wisdom.

b

PHAEDRUS: I join in your prayer, Socrates. If it is better for us that it should be so, then so let it be. But your speech – I've been sitting here for some time wondering how you could construct a speech so much finer than the one before. I'm afraid Lysias will strike me as pretty paltry stuff – that's if he's prepared to enter another speech against it at all. Heaven knows, Socrates, it's not so long since one of our politicians was telling him off and finding

c

fault with him for this practice of his; and all through the telling-off he kept calling him a 'speech-writer'. So we may find that ambition makes Lysias *refuse* to write.

SOCRATES: What a ridiculous idea. Young man, you are quite wrong about your friend if you think him so frightened of a bit of noise. But maybe you believe the person telling him off really meant what he said as a term of reproach.

PHAEDRUS: He certainly *sounded* as if he meant it that way, Socrates. And you yourself must be well aware that the most powerful and respected people in our cities wouldn't dream of writing down their speeches, and leaving their written works behind them. They're afraid of the judgement of later ages, afraid of being called sophists.

SOCRATES: Are you forgetting that people can say one thing and mean the exact opposite? Quite apart from which, you're forgetting that it's the most big-headed of our public figures who are most passionate about writing down their speeches, and about the idea of leaving written works behind them. Every speech they write, they're so taken with the people who support it that the first thing they put in any of their works is the names of their supporters.

PHAEDRUS: What do you mean? I don't understand.

SOCRATES: You mean you don't understand that in anything written by a politician, the first thing you find written is the name of the person who supports it.

PHAEDRUS: Explain.

SOCRATES: Well, the writer says something like 'The council decided', or 'The people decided', or both; and 'So-and-so spoke' – here he names himself with full solemnity, and praises himself to the skies. After that he says his piece, showing off his wisdom to his supporters; sometimes he makes a whole *magnum opus* out of it. Or don't you agree that a work of this kind is just the same as a written speech?

PHAEDRUS: No, I do agree.   b

SOCRATES: Well then, if it gets on to the statute book, its author leaves the theatre well-pleased. But if it is expunged, if he is deprived of his position as a speech-writer and his claim to be an author, then he feels grief, and so do his supporters.

PHAEDRUS: They certainly do.

SOCRATES: Not because they despise the activity, obviously, but because they admire it.

PHAEDRUS: Absolutely.

SOCRATES: What if he becomes a speaker or ruler capable of assuming the power of Lycurgus   c
or Solon or Darius, and gaining immortality in his city as a speech-writer? Doesn't the man himself, in his lifetime, think he is on a par with the gods? And don't those who come after him hold exactly the same opinion of him, when they look at the things he wrote?

PHAEDRUS: They do indeed.

SOCRATES: In which case, do you think anyone like that – no matter who he was, or however hostile to Lysias – is going to blame him just for being a writer?

PHAEDRUS: It's most unlikely, on your argument.

It looks as if he'd be blaming Lysias for what he himself desired.

SOCRATES: So the mere fact of writing speeches, as anyone can see, is not in itself something to be ashamed of.

PHAEDRUS: Why should it be?

SOCRATES: The thing people *should* be ashamed of, in my opinion, is speaking and writing which is not good – which is shameful and bad, in fact.

PHAEDRUS: Obviously.

SOCRATES: What then is the mark of good writing and its opposite? Is this a question on which we should examine Lysias a little, and any other past or future writer, whether he writes for political purposes or private, and whether in the metre of poetry or the prose of everyday life?

PHAEDRUS: Should we examine him? Need you ask? I simply can't imagine anyone finding any point in life at all, other than pleasures of this kind. Certainly not those for which pain is a necessary prelude if you are to feel any pleasure at all – and that means virtually all bodily pleasures. That's why they are quite rightly called slavish.

SOCRATES: Well, we have time on our hands, by all appearances. And besides, I think the cicadas over our heads, singing and talking to one another as they do in the heat, are keeping an eye on us. If they saw us, like most people in the middle of the day, not talking but dozing, falling under their spell out of mental laziness, they would laugh at us – and with good reason. They'd think we were slaves who had wandered into their little retreat like sheep, taking our siesta by the spring. But if they see us

talking, avoiding their spell like sailors sailing past
the Sirens, then perhaps they may be pleased with
us, and grant us that gift which they have from the
gods, and can give to men.

PHAEDRUS: What gift? Something I've never
heard of, I suspect.

SOCRATES: Certainly not the kind of gift a lover
of the Muses should never have heard of. The
story goes that these cicadas were once men, in
the days before there were Muses. When the Muses
were born, and song first made its appearance,
there were those among mankind who were so
overwhelmed by pleasure that, so the story goes,
they forgot all about food and drink as they sang,
and died before they realized what was happening.
It is from them that the race of cicadas subsequently came into existence. And the gift they
received from the Muses was this, that when they
are born they need no food; they start singing
straight away, without food or drink, and continue
till they die. Then they go to the Muses, to report
which of them is honoured here, and which among
men honours them. They tell Terpsichore, for
example, about those who have honoured her in
the dance; that endears those people to her. They
tell Erato who has honoured her in matters of
love; and likewise the others, depending on the
kind of honour due to each. They tell Calliope,
who is the eldest, and Ourania, who comes next,
which people are passing their time in philosophy
and honouring the music of those who, more than
the other Muses, dwell in heaven and in discussion
– divine and human – and whose voice is the

b

c

d

most beautiful. So we have many good reasons for talking, rather than going to sleep, in the middle of the day.

PHAEDRUS: Talk it shall be, then.

SOCRATES: Very well. The question we posed a moment ago, what is the right way to make or compose a speech, and what is the wrong way, is the one we have to examine.

PHAEDRUS: Obviously.

SOCRATES: For a speech to be made well, and in the right way, must it not be the case that the mind of the speaker knows the truth of the things he proposes to talk about?

PHAEDRUS: I have heard an answer to that question, my dear Socrates, and it is this. It is not essential for the man who wants to be an orator to find out what is in reality just, but only what the majority of those who will make up the jury will *think* is just. And again, not what is really good or bad, but only what will be thought so. That is where persuasion originates, not in the truth.

SOCRATES: We should be 'loath to cast away the speech' of the wise, Phaedrus. We must examine what they say closely, to see if there is anything in it. And in this case especially, we should not reject what has just been said.

PHAEDRUS: You're right.

SOCRATES: Here's one way of looking at it.

PHAEDRUS: What way is that?

SOCRATES: Imagine I was trying to persuade you to get a horse, to defend yourself in wartime, but that neither of us knew what a horse was. However, I did at least know one thing about you, which is that Phaedrus believes a horse to be, of all tame animals, the one with the largest ears.

PHAEDRUS: That would be absurd, Socrates.

SOCRATES: Not really. Not until I started eagerly trying to persuade you by composing a speech in praise of the donkey, calling it a horse, and saying what an invaluable asset the creature would be, both for domestic use and on campaign – useful for mounted combat, besides being capable of carrying equipment, and with many other uses besides.

c

PHAEDRUS: At that point it *would* be the height of absurdity.

SOCRATES: Still, better an absurd friend than a clever enemy, surely?

PHAEDRUS: On the face of it, yes.

SOCRATES: Now, take an expert in rhetoric who doesn't know good from evil, and who finds his city in the same position. When he tries to persuade them, it isn't a question of his praising some wretched donkey as if it were a horse, but rather of speaking about evil as if it were good. And if he has made a study of what most people think, and succeeds in persuading the people to do evil instead of good, what harvest do you think rhetoric then reaps from what it has sown?

d

PHAEDRUS: A very poor one.

SOCRATES: Now, my good Phaedrus, have we been too crude in our criticism of the science of speaking? 'For heaven's sake,' she might say in her defence, 'why do you talk such nonsense? I do not compel anyone who is ignorant of the truth to learn the art of speaking. No, if I have any advice for him, it is to acquire truth first, and then grasp hold of me. One thing I would stress, however: without me, the man who does know what is will still be wholly incapable of persuading scientifically.'

e   PHAEDRUS: Will she be justified in making this claim?

SOCRATES: Yes, but only if the arguments attacking her support her claim to be a science. I fancy I can hear some of them coming forward and making a sworn statement that she is lying, that she is not a science, simply a knack. Nothing scientific at all. Of speaking, as they say in Laconia, there is in sooth no science, nor will there ever be, without a grasp of truth.

261   PHAEDRUS: These are important arguments, Socrates. Bring them before us. Examine their case, and the way they present it.

SOCRATES: Come forward, my fine creatures. Persuade Phaedrus, who is so fortunate in his off-spring, that without an adequate grasp of philosophy he will never become an adequate speaker about anything. Let Phaedrus give you your answers.

PHAEDRUS: Ask your questions.

SOCRATES: Very well. Might not the science of rhetoric, in general, be some sort of leading of the soul by means of what is spoken? I don't just mean in the courts, or any other kind of public gathering. I'm thinking of private discussions too. Rhetoric

b   is the same, whether its subject is unimportant or important. Rightly considered, it is of no more value in a serious context than a trivial one. Is that roughly what you've been told?

PHAEDRUS: Good god, no. Quite the opposite. Scientific speaking and writing is pretty much confined to the lawcourts, I would say; and speaking, just by itself, to politics. I haven't heard of any wider application.

SOCRATES: Really? Have you heard only of Nestor's *Science of Rhetoric*, and Odysseus', the ones they wrote in those quiet moments at Troy? You haven't heard of the things Palamedes wrote?

PHAEDRUS: Heavens, no. Nor have I heard   c
of the things Nestor wrote, unless you're casting Gorgias in the role of Nestor, with someone like Thrasymachus or Theodorus as Odysseus.

SOCRATES: Perhaps I am. Anyway, never mind them. Tell me this: in the lawcourts, what is it the opposing parties do? Don't they simply make opposing speeches? What else can we call it?

PHAEDRUS: No, that is what they do.

SOCRATES: About what is just and what is unjust?

PHAEDRUS: Yes.

SOCRATES: And will the person who does this in a scientific way make the same people regard the same things first as just, and then, when he chooses,   d
as unjust?

PHAEDRUS: Of course.

SOCRATES: And in political speeches as well, will he make the city regard the same things as first good, and then again later as the opposite?

PHAEDRUS: He will.

SOCRATES: Aren't we well aware that the Palamedes who comes from Elea speaks scientifically, making it seem to his hearers that the same things are like and unlike, or one and many, or again at rest and in motion?

PHAEDRUS: We are. Very well aware.

SOCRATES: So the making of opposing speeches is not confined to the courts and political life. There is, apparently, this one single science – if it is a science – which covers speaking of all kinds. With its help you can liken any possible subject of comparison to any possible object of comparison. And if anyone else likens one thing to another, and conceals the fact, you can bring this to light.

PHAEDRUS: What kind of thing are you talking about?

SOCRATES: I think it will become clear if we ask ourselves this question: does deception occur more readily when things are very different, or when they are slightly different?

PHAEDRUS: When they are slightly different.

SOCRATES: And if you are changing your ground from one position to its opposite, are you more likely to get away with it step by step than in one big jump?

PHAEDRUS: Obviously.

SOCRATES: So if a man wants to deceive someone else, and not be deceived himself, he needs a precise knowledge of the likeness and unlikeness of the things which are.

PHAEDRUS: Yes, he's bound to.

SOCRATES: And if he doesn't know the truth of each thing, will he be able to discern in other things the likeness, great or small, to the thing he doesn't know about?

PHAEDRUS: No, that's not possible.   b

SOCRATES: For those whose beliefs run counter to the way things are, then – those who are deceived – it is clear that this state of ignorance stole upon them gradually, as the result of likenesses of various sorts.

PHAEDRUS: Yes, that is how it arises.

SOCRATES: Is it possible, in that case, for a man to be skilled at sidetracking others – using these similarities, on any occasion, to lead them gradually from what is to its opposite – or at avoiding this himself, without having first recognized what each of the things that is really is?

PHAEDRUS: No, never.

SOCRATES: In which case, my friend, the science   c
of speaking offered by the man who does not know the truth, but who has been chasing after things as they seem to be, will be somewhat laughable and unscientific.

PHAEDRUS: Very likely.

SOCRATES: Would you like us to look at that speech of Lysias' which you have there, and the ones we made ourselves, and find in them some-thing of the characteristics we call unscientific and scientific?

PHAEDRUS: I can think of nothing I'd like better. At the moment our discussion is a bit bald; we need better examples.

SOCRATES: What is more, the two speeches delivered do, by some chance, afford an example of someone who knows the truth misleading his   d
hearers by not being serious in what he says. For my part, Phaedrus, I blame the gods of this place;

though it may also be that the Muses' spokesmen, these singers over our heads, have breathed this gift upon us, since I for one claim no share in any science of speaking.

PHAEDRUS: I'll let that go. Just explain what you are talking about.

SOCRATES: Very well. Read me the opening of Lysias' speech.

e   PHAEDRUS: 'You know how things are with me, and you have heard me explain why I think it would be a good thing for us that this should happen. I don't think the fact of my not being your lover should stop me getting what I want. Lovers, when their desire cools, regret the . . .'

SOCRATES: Stop there. We have to point out where Lysias goes wrong, and where the speech is unscientifically constructed. Isn't that right?

263   PHAEDRUS: Yes.

SOCRATES: Isn't there one point, at any rate, which is plain to everyone? With topics of this kind, aren't we of one mind about some things, and completely at odds over others?

PHAEDRUS: I think I can see what you are getting at. But give me a bit more of an explanation, all the same.

SOCRATES: When somebody uses the word 'iron', or 'silver', it means the same thing to all of us, doesn't it?

PHAEDRUS: Yes, of course.

SOCRATES: What about 'just' or 'good'? Doesn't each person go his own way? Don't we disagree with one another, and even with ourselves?

PHAEDRUS: We certainly do.

SOCRATES: So in some cases we agree, and in   b
others we don't.

PHAEDRUS: Yes.

SOCRATES: In which of the two situations, then,
are we more easily deceived? In which does rhetoric
have the greater power?

PHAEDRUS: Obviously, the times when we all
go our separate ways.

SOCRATES: So anyone who aims to follow a
science of rhetoric must in the first place have made
a systematic classification of these categories; he
must have laid hold of some distinguishing mark
for each class – the one in which most people neces
sarily go their own way, and the one in which they
don't.

PHAEDRUS: That really *would* be a fine piece of   c
classification for him to have mastered, Socrates, if
he could lay hold of that.

SOCRATES: Secondly, in everything he ap
proaches, he must be very alert, keeping a sharp
lookout to see which of the two categories the thing
he wants to talk about in fact belongs in.

PHAEDRUS: Of course.

SOCRATES: What about love? Which of the two
classes are we to put that in? Is it one of the things
we disagree about or agree about?

PHAEDRUS: Disagree about, I should imagine.
How else do you suppose it could have been pos
sible for you to describe it as you just have described
it? You said that it meant harm to the one loved and
the one loving, but then again that it was in fact the
greatest of blessings.

SOCRATES: You are absolutely right. Now, tell   d

me one more thing – I was so carried away myself,
I really can't remember. Did I give a definition of
love at the start of my speech?

PHAEDRUS: You certainly did – you made a real
meal of it.

SOCRATES: Ah! That's how much more scientific you say the Nymphs, daughters of Achelous,
are when it comes to speaking, and Pan, the son of
Hermes, than Lysias the son of Cephalus. Or have
I got it wrong? Did Lysias also, in the opening of
his speech on love, insist that we take love as one
single existing thing, defined by him? Did he then
look to this definition as he constructed the whole
speech that followed, right through to its conclusion? Would you like us to read the opening of it
again?

PHAEDRUS: We could, to please you. But the
thing you want is not there.

SOCRATES: Let's have it anyway. I want to hear
the man himself.

PHAEDRUS: 'You know how things are with me,
and you have heard me explain why I think it would
be a good thing for us that this should happen. I
don't think the fact of my not being your lover
should stop me getting what I want. Lovers, when
their desire cools, regret the benefits they have
conferred...'

SOCRATES: He really does seem to be a long way
from doing what we want. He doesn't even begin
at the beginning. He begins at the end, trying to go
through it in the wrong direction, like a swimmer
swimming on his back, and starting with what
a lover would normally say to his boyfriend right

at the end. Am I wrong, dear Phaedrus, light of my life?

PHAEDRUS: Well, his whole speech certainly b does have *an* end in view, Socrates.

SOCRATES: How about the rest of it? Don't you feel that the parts of the speech have been chucked together all higgledy-piggledy? Do you think the second thing he says had to be put second for some compelling reason? Or any of the other things he says? I'm no expert, but I got the impression that what was so bravely said was simply the first thing that came into the writer's head. How about you? Are you aware of some unbreakable rule of speech-writing which would make him put these particular items together in this particular order?

PHAEDRUS: I'm flattered that you should regard me as capable of analysing his methods so c precisely.

SOCRATES: Well, there is at any rate one thing I think you would admit: any speech should be like an animal in the way it is put together. It must have some sort of body, all its own; it must not be without a head, or without feet; it must have a middle and extremities, written in such a way as to harmonize with one another and with the whole.

PHAEDRUS: Yes, obviously.

SOCRATES: Very well. Now see if your friend's speech is like that, or not. You'll find it exactly like the inscription written, as some say, on the head-stone of Midas, king of Phrygia.

PHAEDRUS: What inscription? And what is d special about it?

SOCRATES: It goes like this:

> A maid of bronze, on Midas' grave I lie,
> While river-waters flow, and trees grow high,
> Remaining here on his lamented tomb,
> Telling the passing world of Midas' doom.

e Any of the lines can come first or last, as I expect you've noticed, without it making any difference.

PHAEDRUS: Now you're making fun of our speech, Socrates.

SOCRATES: Very well, let's leave it. I don't want to upset you – although I do think it contains plenty of examples which it would be helpful to look at, though certainly not to try and imitate. Let's move on to the other speeches. They contained something, I believe, which anyone wanting to make a study of speeches ought to look at.

265 PHAEDRUS: What kind of thing?

SOCRATES: The two speeches were opposites, I take it. One said you should grant your favours to a lover, the other that you should grant them to someone who was not a lover.

PHAEDRUS: And spoken like a man, in both cases. Manly, in fact.

SOCRATES: I thought for a moment you were going to say 'madly', which would have been the exact truth. The very word I was looking for. We did say, didn't we, that love was a kind of madness.

PHAEDRUS: Yes.

SOCRATES: And that madness was of two kinds – one arising from human illness, the other from a divinely inspired alteration to our normal behaviour.

PHAEDRUS: We did indeed.   b

SOCRATES: And of the supernatural madness we distinguished four parts, the work of four gods; we attributed prophecy to the inspiration of Apollo, ecstatic madness to Dionysus, creativity to the Muses, and the fourth kind to Aphrodite and Eros; and we said that the madness of love, erotic love, was the finest. We also painted some sort of picture of the experience of what it is like to be in love. Maybe we touched on the truth a bit, but then again, perhaps we were led astray as well. We combined all this into a reasonably convincing speech, and sang a song of praise, in the form of a myth – light-   c hearted, but sober and respectful – to your master, Phaedrus, and mine, to Eros, the protector of beautiful boys.

PHAEDRUS: We did. And as far as I'm concerned, it was a pleasure to listen to.

SOCRATES: In which case, let's pick up one point from it – the way the speech was able to switch from criticism to approval.

PHAEDRUS: Very well. How do you explain that?

SOCRATES: In my view, most of the speech was really in fun – just for entertainment. But almost by chance a distinction was made between two things; it would be satisfying to get a scientific grasp of   d their importance.

PHAEDRUS: What things?

SOCRATES: One is taking the overall view, bringing together under one heading things which are widely separated, with a view to defining each one, and making clear what it is that is being explained. Take our definition just now of what love is. The speech may have been a good one or a bad one, but at least it was able, using this method, to say something that was clear and without contradiction.

PHAEDRUS: And the second thing, Socrates?

e   SOCRATES: The ability to chop things up into their forms again, following the natural joints or connections, and not trying, like an incompetent butcher, to split any of the parts. For example, the two speeches we have just made took the irrational part of the mind as a single common form. Just as

266 parts of the body come in pairs, with the same name, and are called left and right, so the two speeches treated this question of madness as being naturally a single form in us. The first speech separated off the left-hand form, and went on subdividing that until it found among the pieces a love which was in some way 'cack-handed'. It had harsh words for this love, quite rightly. The second speech took us to the parts of madness on the right-hand side, finding there a love with the same name, but this time some- how divinely inspired. Holding it up for us to see, it

b   praised it as the cause of our greatest blessings.

PHAEDRUS: That's exactly right.

SOCRATES: For my part, Phaedrus, I've always had a great love for these techniques of dividing and bringing together. They help me in my speaking and in my thinking. And if someone seems to me to have been born with the ability to see things in their unity and diversity, then 'close behind I follow in his track, as if he were a god'. What is more, I have a name for those who have this ability. Up to now I have called them dialecticians, though whether that is the right term or not, god only

knows. But what should we call them now, if we   c
take advice from you and Lysias? Tell me that. Or is
this ability simply that science of speaking through
which Thrasymachus and the rest have become
wise themselves, and can also make wise anyone
who is prepared to pay them a king's ransom?

PHAEDRUS: Well, kingly they may be, but they
certainly don't have knowledge of the things you
are asking about. For that kind of thing, I think the
term you have chosen, dialectical, is the right one.
But as for rhetoric, I think we have yet to put our
finger on it.

SOCRATES: Really? Can there be something   d
good which has nothing to do with dialectic, but
which is nevertheless grasped scientifically? We
must treat it with all respect, if so, and say what on
earth it is, this left-out part of rhetoric.

PHAEDRUS: There must be dozens, Socrates.
Just look at the contents of the books on the science
of speaking.

SOCRATES: Ah yes. Thank you for reminding
me. The Introductory Remarks have to come first,
I believe, at the beginning of the speech. That's
what you're referring to, isn't it? The 'finer points'
of the science?

PHAEDRUS: Yes.   e

SOCRATES: Next must be a Statement of the
Case, with Accompanying Evidence. The third item
is Proofs, and the fourth is Probabilities. Then
Assurance and Reassurance. I'm sure the great
Byzantine wordsmith mentions those.

PHAEDRUS: You mean the excellent Theodorus?

SOCRATES: Of course. Then there are the

267 Refutation and Additional Refutation, which he says must be included in a speech for the prosecution or the defence. And surely we should bring forward the worthy citizen of Paros, Evenus – the inventor of Insinuation and the Compliment in Passing. Some people attribute the Insult in Passing to him as well. In verse, just to make it easier to remember. What a talent! Let us not disturb the sleep of Tisias or Gorgias, however, with their recognition that probabilities are more valuable than truth, their ability, by the power of argument, to make the trivial seem important and the important seem trivial, and to express what is novel in a

b traditional way, and its opposite in a novel way, and their discovery of conciseness and interminable longwindedness on all subjects. Prodicus heard me say that once. He laughed. He said he was the only person to have discovered what is wanted in a speech – neither long nor short, but just the right length.

PHAEDRUS: Prodicus, you're a genius!

SOCRATES: And are we going to leave Hippias out? I imagine our friend from Elis would vote the same way as Prodicus.

PHAEDRUS: Naturally.

SOCRATES: And what mention are we to make of Polus' *Treasurehouse of Terms* – Speaking with

c Reduplication, Speaking in Maxims, Speaking in Similes and the like – or of Licymnius' *Definitions*, which he presented to Polus as his contribution to the art of fine writing?

PHAEDRUS: And weren't there things like this in Protagoras' works, Socrates?

SOCRATES: Yes, indeed, my dear boy. Something called Verbal Precision, and many other points of good style. Then there's the Science of Lamentation – long-drawn-out speeches on old age and poverty. The master of these, in my view, is our doughty hero from Chalcedon. A specialist also, this fellow, in rousing a crowd to anger, then putting a spell on them and, in his own words, charming them out of their anger again. As for abuse, whether handing it out or warding it off, wherever it comes from, he is the master. And when it comes to the ending of speeches, they all seem to be in agreement. Some people call it Recapitulation; others give it a variety of names.

d

PHAEDRUS: You mean reminding the listeners at the end, in a summary, of all the points which have been made?

SOCRATES: Yes, that's what I mean. Plus anything else you can think of to do with the science of speaking.

PHAEDRUS: Only details. Nothing worth discussing.

SOCRATES: Very well. Let's not bother with details. I'd like to look more closely at the things we've got so far, and see just what there is of scientific force in them.

268

PHAEDRUS: A very powerful force, Socrates – at least at public meetings.

SOCRATES: Yes, it is powerful. But for heaven's sake, Phaedrus, you've got eyes, the same as I have. Don't you also find, as I do, one or two gaping holes in the fabric?

PHAEDRUS: I wish you'd point them out to me.

SOCRATES: Tell me this then. Suppose someone went up to your friend Eryximachus, or his father Acumenus, and said, 'I know how to treat the body. I can heat it, if I so wish, or I can cool it down. I can make it vomit, if I choose, or again, open the bowels. All that sort of thing. On the strength of this knowledge I maintain that I am a medical expert, and that I can make a medical expert out of anyone to whom I pass on this knowledge.' What do you think their reaction to this claim would be?

PHAEDRUS: Well, obviously they'd ask him if he also knew who he should prescribe each of these treatments to, under what conditions, and up to what limit.

SOCRATES: And suppose he said, 'I've no idea. I expect any pupil of mine to be capable of doing the things you are asking about for himself.' What then?

PHAEDRUS: They'd say the man was mad, I should think. He might *think* he was a doctor, after reading about it in a book somewhere, or coming across a few common prescriptions, but in fact he knew nothing of medicine at all.

SOCRATES: Or again, suppose someone went up to Sophocles or Euripides, and said he knew how to construct immensely long speeches about practically nothing, or really short ones about what was important – or speeches full of pathos, if he chose, or again, by contrast, ones which were alarming and menacing. And so on and so forth. Suppose he said he thought that what he was passing on when he taught these things was the art of tragedy?

PHAEDRUS: Again, I think they'd laugh at him, Socrates, at the idea that tragedy was anything other than the proper arrangement of these elements so as to fit in both with one another and with the whole work.

SOCRATES: And yet I don't think they'd descend to vulgar abuse. It would be more like a musician coming across someone who thought himself an expert on harmony because he did in fact know how to produce the top note and bottom note on a stringed instrument. He wouldn't be too savage with him: 'You're out of your mind, you poor fool!' No, he'd be more considerate, as you'd expect a friend of the Muses to be: 'My friend, that knowledge is indeed one of the prerequisites for anyone who is going to be an expert in harmony; yet it is perfectly possible for someone with this ability still to know absolutely nothing about harmony. What you know are the essential preliminaries to harmony, not harmony itself.'   e

PHAEDRUS: Absolutely right.

SOCRATES: Equally, Sophocles could say that   269 the person who was showing off to him and Euripides knew the essential preliminaries to tragedy, but not tragedy itself; and Acumenus, that they knew the essential preliminaries to medicine, but not medicine itself.

PHAEDRUS: Indeed they could.

SOCRATES: And what about the honey-tongued Adrastus? Or Pericles, for that matter? Imagine them listening to the 'finer points of style' we have just been listing – all the Concisenesses and Likenesses and what have you – our list which we said we should examine in the clear light of day. Do we think their reaction would be as harsh as yours and   b

mine? Would they, out of sheer vulgarity, direct
some crass remark at those who offer that sort of
thing, in their writings and teachings, as if it were a
science of rhetoric? Or would they, being wiser than
us, rebuke us as well, and say: 'Phaedrus and Socrates, if people with no knowledge of dialectic are
incapable of defining exactly what rhetoric is, you
should not be angry, but forgiving; it is this inability
which causes them to think, once they have the
knowledge which is an essential preliminary to the
science, that they have discovered rhetoric itself,
and to believe, when they teach this knowledge to
others, that they have given a complete course in
rhetoric – as if putting it all across in a convincing
manner, together with the trivial matter of organ-
izing the speech as a whole, are things which their
pupils in their speeches must provide from their
own resources.'

PHAEDRUS: Well, Socrates, I suppose that probably is the reality of the science which these teachers
and writers offer as rhetoric. I for one think you are
right about that. But then how – and from where –
might anyone be able to acquire the science of the
real expert in rhetoric, the true orator?

SOCRATES: If it's the ability you are interested
in, Phaedrus, the ability to become the perfect per-
former, this will probably – I might even say necessarily – be like anything else. If you have a natural
aptitude for rhetoric, then you will be a distinguished orator, provided you gain knowledge
and experience in addition. But if you are deficient
in any part of these, you will be to that extent incomplete. As for its being a science, well, I do not think

the path trodden by Lysias and Thrasymachus is the right approach.

PHAEDRUS: What is the right approach, then?

SOCRATES: Well, my fine Phaedrus, it looks as if e there may have been some good reason why Pericles was the most accomplished of them all when it came to rhetoric.

PHAEDRUS: Why so?

SOCRATES: Without exception, the most important of the sciences make a further demand, for an approach to nature based on windbaggery and 270 stargazing. The requisite loftiness of intellect and general omnicompetence seem to have their origin in some such source. It's certainly something Pericles acquired, over and above his natural talent. I think it came from being involved with Anaxagoras, who was very much of that stamp. This gave Pericles his fill of stargazing, until he arrived at the very nature of mind and non-mind, the subjects of so much of Anaxagoras' talk. Pericles drew on this, for his science of speaking, whatever was relevant to it.

PHAEDRUS: How do you mean?

SOCRATES: The approach taken by the science b of medicine is the same, I take it, as that taken by rhetoric.

PHAEDRUS: In what way?

SOCRATES: In both there is a need to distinguish the nature of something – of body in the one case, of soul in the other – if you intend to be scientific, and not work solely by rule of thumb and past experience. For the body, the aim is to bring health and vigour by prescribing drugs and diet. For the soul, the prescription is words and rules of

behaviour, and the aim is to impart whatever con-
victions and moral goodness you wish to impart.

PHAEDRUS: Very likely so, Socrates.

c   SOCRATES: In which case, do you think it is
possible to get any worthwhile understanding of the
nature of soul without understanding it as a whole?

PHAEDRUS: No, and if we are to have any con-
fidence in Hippocrates, the follower of Asclepius,
there can't even be an understanding of the body
without such an approach.

SOCRATES: He is right, my friend. All the same,
in addition to Hippocrates, we should study the
argument closely, to see if it agrees.

PHAEDRUS: Yes.

SOCRATES: Very well. What exactly is it, then,
that Hippocrates and the correct argument say
about nature? Shouldn't thinking about the nature

d   of anything at all be done like this? First, is it simple
or complex, this thing about which we are going
to be scientific ourselves, and able to make others
scientific? Second, if it is simple, we should ask
what capacity it has for acting – and on what. What
capacity for being acted upon – and by what. If it
has several forms, we should enumerate them, and
see for each one, as we did for the single form,
which it is its nature to act with – and what action it
will take. And what it is its nature to be acted upon
by – and what action, and through what agency.

PHAEDRUS: I dare say, Socrates.

SOCRATES: Certainly any approach which didn't
ask these questions would look like the blind lead-
e   ing the blind; and on no account should we compare
the scientific enquirer into anything to a person who

is blind or deaf. If one person puts words across to another in a scientific way, he is clearly doing no more than demonstrate the essential nature of the thing to which those words will be directed. And that thing, I take it, will be soul.

PHAEDRUS: Of course.

SOCRATES: In which case, his efforts are directed   271
to this end in their entirety, since this is where he is trying to create persuasion, is it not?

PHAEDRUS: Yes.

SOCRATES: Obviously, then, if Thrasymachus or anyone else is serious about teaching the science of rhetoric, in the first place he will write with complete precision, allowing us to see whether the soul is by its nature a single, uniform thing, or of many forms, like the shape of the body. This is what we mean, after all, by demonstrating the nature of something.

PHAEDRUS: It is indeed.

SOCRATES: Secondly, he will show with which form it naturally acts, or is acted upon by something else, and what the action is.

PHAEDRUS: True. What then?

SOCRATES: Thirdly, he will draw up a classifi-   b
cation of the types of speech and soul, and the effect one has on the other; and he will run through all the various causes, matching speech to effect in each case, and explaining what kind of soul, as a result of what kind of speech, will in one case necessarily be convinced, and in another not be convinced – and for what reason.

PHAEDRUS: Yes, that would certainly be the best way, by the looks of it.

SOCRATES: And no speech given in any other way, my friend, whether written as an exercise or actually delivered, will ever be delivered or written scientifically. Not on any other subject, and not on

c   this one either. The people who now write on the techniques of rhetoric, the ones you have heard, are unscrupulous enough to keep quiet about this, though they know all about soul. So until they speak and write in this way, let us not accept their claim to be scientific writers.

PHAEDRUS: What way is that?

SOCRATES: Well, it is not an easy matter to give the precise words. But I don't mind saying *along what lines* you should write if you want to be as scientific as the nature of the activity permits.

PHAEDRUS: Very well, say that.

SOCRATES: Since the function of speech is actually to lead the soul, it is essential that the would-be

d   orator knows what forms soul has: their number is so and so, and their nature such and such, which is why some people are of one kind and others of another kind. And once we have distinguished the kinds of soul in this way, then the forms of speech in turn are so and so many in number, each of the appropriate type. People of one kind are for this reason easily persuaded in one direction by speeches of one sort, and people of a different kind not easily persuaded by the same sort. The orator must have a good understanding of these things, and must next observe their actions and effects in

e   the real world. He must have the ability to follow them with keen perception; otherwise there will be at this point no further advantage to him from the arguments he heard in my company. But when he is both capable of saying what kind of man will be persuaded by what kinds of things, and has the capacity to recognize him when he is there, and point out to himself that this is the man, and this the nature, which was talked about earlier – that it is here before him now, in real life, and that it is for him to apply *these* speeches, in *this* way, to bring about persuasion of *this* kind; once he has mastered all this, and developed in addition a good sense of when to speak and when to be silent, when to use brevity, pathos, exaggeration, and all the types of speech in his repertoire – being able to judge the right and wrong times for them – then and only then is his scientific knowledge well and truly completed. If he is deficient in any of these, in his speaking or teaching or writing, and yet claims to speak scientifically, then the person who doesn't believe him is in a very strong position. 'Well, Phaedrus and Socrates,' our author might say to us, 'do you agree? Or should we accept some other account of the science of speaking?'

PHAEDRUS: No, Socrates. Any other account is out of the question. But it seems no small undertaking.

SOCRATES: True. That is why we should turn all our arguments inside out, to see if any shorter or easier way is going to make its appearance somewhere, and save us taking a long, steep, out-of-the-way route to no purpose, when we could have taken a short, level one instead. If you have any suggestion at all, something you've heard from Lysias or anyone else, try to remember it, and tell me.

272

b

c

PHAEDRUS: If it were just a question of trying, I would. But it isn't. I really can't help.

SOCRATES: Do you want me to say something, then – something I've heard from some of the people who know about these things?

PHAEDRUS: Yes, of course.

SOCRATES: Well, Phaedrus, it is said to be right to give the devil his due.

d   PHAEDRUS: Then you too must do that.

SOCRATES: Very well. They say there is no need to take all this so seriously, or go miles out of our way to take it back to first principles. It's exactly as we said, at the beginning of this discussion: the man who wants to be any good at rhetoric need have nothing to do with the truth of things just or things good, or for that matter of men who are just and good, either by nature or by upbringing. In the law-courts nobody has the slightest interest in the truth of these things, only in what is persuasive. This

e   means what is probable, which is what the person who is going to speak scientifically must concentrate on. There are even times when you shouldn't say what really happened at all, if it happened in an improbable way. Instead you should say what is probable. This applies both to the prosecution and the defence, and in any kind of speech at all, what is probable is what is to be followed, though that often means saying goodbye to the truth. If this is done

273   throughout the whole speech, that gives us the complete science.

PHAEDRUS: What you've described, Socrates, is exactly the claim made by those who have scientific pretensions in their approach to speaking. I remember now that we briefly touched on this kind of thing earlier on. It does seem to be something of great importance to those who are interested in these things.

SOCRATES: But surely ... Well, take Tisias himself – you've been through his work with a toothcomb, so why not let Tisias instruct us on this point too? Doesn't he say that what is probable is just what most people think?

PHAEDRUS: Yes, simply that.

SOCRATES: And it was this clever scientific discovery, apparently, which made him say that if a man who is weak but courageous beats up a man who is strong but cowardly, steals his cloak or something of his, and is taken to court, then neither of them should tell the truth. The coward should not admit that he was beaten up by the brave man on his own, while the other should establish that the two of them *were* on their own, and then use the classic 'Would a man like me attack a man like him?' The plaintiff will certainly not admit his cowardice, but will try to invent some falsehood instead – perhaps giving his opponent the chance to prove him wrong. And in other situations, too, scientific speaking will be more or less of this kind. Isn't that what he says, Phaedrus?

PHAEDRUS: Indeed it is.

SOCRATES: Phew! It certainly looks like a cunningly concealed science Tisias has discovered – or whoever it actually was, and whatever he is proud to take his name from. All the same, my friend, I wonder whether we should or should not say to him ...

d   PHAEDRUS: What?

SOCRATES: 'As it happens, Tisias, we've been saying for a little while now, before you turned up, that for most people this idea of what is probable arises out of some kind of similarity to the truth. And we've just explained that without exception it is the person who knows the truth who has the best idea how to recognize these similarities. So if you have something more to say about a science of speaking, we'd be glad to hear it. Otherwise we'll put our faith in the explanation we gave just now –

e   that unless a man can enumerate the natures of those who are going to hear him, and has the ability to classify the things that are according to their forms, and include each individual thing under a single category, he will never achieve whatever level of expertise in speaking is possible for a human being. The only way to gain this ability is by a lot of hard work, which a man should undertake, if he has any sense, not with a view to human speech and action, but rather that he may be able to speak what is pleasing to the gods, and act in all things, to the best of his ability, in a way which is pleasing to them. There is after all no need, Tisias, according to those who are wiser than us, for anyone with any sense to

274   work at pleasing his fellow-slaves – except incidentally – but only his masters, who are good both in themselves and in their origin. So if the journey is long and circuitous, do not be surprised. It is for reasons of great importance that we make this detour, not for what you have in mind – though that too, if it is what you want, will best come about, so our argument claims, as a result of that approach.'

PHAEDRUS: That seems to me to be a counsel of perfection, Socrates. If only we were up to it.

SOCRATES: But if you even attempt what is good, then whatever turns out to happen to you, it will be good that it should happen to you.

b

PHAEDRUS: Very true.

SOCRATES: Very well then, on the scientific and unscientific nature of speaking, let that be enough.

PHAEDRUS: By all means.

SOCRATES: That leaves, does it not, the question of writing. Is it appropriate or inappropriate? When can it rightly be done, and when is it inappropriate?

PHAEDRUS: Yes.

SOCRATES: Do you know how you can best please god, when it comes to speeches, in what you do and what you say?

PHAEDRUS: No. Do you?

SOCRATES: I can at any rate give you a bit of hearsay, from those who have gone before us. As for the truth of it, that is something only they know. But if we could make the same discovery for ourselves, would we any longer care about the fancies of mankind?

c

PHAEDRUS: What an absurd question. Tell me this story you say you have heard.

SOCRATES: Very well. What I heard was this. At Naucratis in Egypt there was one of the ancient gods of that country, whose sacred bird was the one they call the ibis. The name of this spirit was Theuth. He was the first to discover number and arithmetic, geometry and astronomy, besides draughts and dice, and in particular writing. The king of all Egypt at this time was Thamus, in the great city of upper

d

Egypt, which the Greeks call the Egyptian Thebes.
Their name for Thamus is Ammon. Theuth came
to him and showed him his scientific discoveries,
saying they should be passed on to all the Egyptians.
Thamus asked him what use each of them was;
and when Theuth explained, he criticized or praised
e   whatever he disagreed or agreed with. Theuth had
a lot to say about each of his discoveries, so the
story goes, for and against. To give a full account
of them would be a major work. When he came to
writing, however, Theuth said: 'Now this, O king,
is a skill which will make the Egyptians wiser and
better at remembering things. It is an elixir of memory and wisdom.' Thamus' reply was this: 'Theuth,
most scientific of men, it takes one sort of man to
father a science, another to judge what measure of
harm or benefit it brings to those who are going to
use it. So it is in this case. You are the father of
275   writing, and your fondness for it makes you completely mistaken about its effect. This is something
which will produce forgetfulness in the minds of
those who learn it, through disuse of memory. Their
reliance on writing will make them look for external
reminders, in marks made by other people, rather
than their own internal reminders, in themselves. It
is therefore not an elixir of memory you have found,
but of reminding. To those who learn it you offer
the appearance of wisdom, but not the reality. They
will become acquainted with many things without
being taught about them, and so they will seem to
b   know much, when in fact for the most part they
know nothing. Wise-seeming rather than wise, they
will be awkward people to deal with.'

PHAEDRUS 173

PHAEDRUS: You're always inventing stories, Socrates, from Egypt or anywhere else that takes your fancy.

SOCRATES: At the temple of Zeus at Dodona, my friend, they said that the words of an oak tree formed the first prophecies. The people of those times were not so wise as you people of today; it was enough for them, in their simplicity, to listen to oak and rock – just as long as they spoke the truth. To you, perhaps, it makes a difference who the speaker is and where he comes from. You are not solely concerned with whether it is so or not so.

PHAEDRUS: I accept your rebuke. And on the subject of writing, I agree with what your Theban said.

SOCRATES: In which case, if a man thinks he is handing down a science in writing, or if the recipient in turn thinks something clear and certain will emerge from what is written, then he would be full of foolishness, and truly ignorant of Ammon's prophecy, if he thought that written words were anything more than a reminder, to one who knows, of the things the writing is about.

PHAEDRUS: Absolutely right.

SOCRATES: Yes, Phaedrus, because writing has this strange property, I take it, which makes it really very like painting. The things painting produces stand there as if they were alive, but ask them a question, and there's a deathly silence. It's the same with writing. You might think the words spoke with some intelligence; but if you want to know more, and ask them any question about what they say, all they can do is signify the same one thing, over and

over again. Once it is written, any piece of work can
be wheeled around all over the place, alike to those
who know about it and then, in precisely the same
form, to those for whom it is completely irrelevant.
It has no way of speaking to those it should speak
to, and not speaking to those it should not speak
to. And if it gets into difficulties, and is unfairly
criticized, it always needs its father to stand up for
it. It cannot, of its own accord, defend itself or stand
up for itself.

PHAEDRUS: Absolutely right again.

SOCRATES: What about a different way of
speaking? Can we see one which is the more legitimate brother to this? Can we see how it originates,
and how much better and more powerful it is by
nature than the other?

PHAEDRUS: What is this way of speaking, in your
view? What is its origin?

SOCRATES: The one which is written, together
with knowledge, in the soul of him who learns it,
which has the ability to defend itself, and which
knows how to speak to the people it should speak
to and be silent to the people it should be silent to.

PHAEDRUS: You mean the speech of the man
who knows, living and vital, of which the written
version should rightly be called an image or
phantom.

SOCRATES: Quite right. Now, tell me something.
What would a sensible farmer do, if he had seeds he
valued and wanted to bear fruit? Would he in all
seriousness sow them in midsummer, in window-
boxes, and enjoy seeing them in all their glory after
eight days? Or would he do this for fun, for some

special occasion, if he did it at all? For things he was serious about, wouldn't he farm more scientifically, sowing at the right time of year, and being quite happy if what he had sown came to maturity in the eighth month?

PHAEDRUS: That's about right, Socrates. One is   c the way he'd behave if he were serious; the other is how he'd act if he were going about it quite differently, in the way you mention.

SOCRATES: And are we to say that the man who has knowledge of things which are just, excellent and good is less sensible, in his treatment of his seeds, than the farmer?

PHAEDRUS: Emphatically not.

SOCRATES: In which case, he won't, in all seriousness, write them in water – sowing with a pen, in black ink – using words which have no power to stand up for themselves in argument, and no power to teach the truth adequately.

PHAEDRUS: In all probability not.

SOCRATES: Certainly not. His 'literary window-   d boxes', by the looks of it, are what he will sow and write, when he does write, for fun, laying up a treasure-house of reminders both for himself, when he comes to the 'age of forgetfulness', and for anyone else following the same path. It will give him pleasure to watch their young shoots growing. When other people amuse themselves, in a variety of ways – keeping themselves well watered with parties and suchlike activities – it looks as if this man will pass his time instead in the amusements I have described.

PHAEDRUS: You're putting a fine form of   e

amusement side by side with a trivial one, Socrates
– the ability to amuse oneself with words, telling
stories of justice and the other things you've been
talking about.

SOCRATES: Yes, my dear Phaedrus, it is a fine
form of amusement. Far finer, however, in my opinion, is a serious approach to these things, using the
science of dialectic, and finding a receptive soul in
which to plant and sow words which are accom-
panied by knowledge. These words are capable
of standing up for themselves and the man who
planted them; they are not without fruit, but contain
a seed from which all sorts of words take root in all
sorts of natures. In this way they can make it immortal for all time, and its possessor happy to the fullest
extent possible for a human being.

PHAEDRUS: Yes, that is finer still, what you
describe.

SOCRATES: In that case, Phaedrus, we are now
in a position to decide those earlier questions, since
we are agreed on these.

PHAEDRUS: Which questions?

SOCRATES: The ones whose examination led us
to the point we have now arrived at. What were we
to make of the criticism of Lysias for writing his
speeches? And of the speeches themselves, which
of them were written scientifically and which unscientifically? What is scientific and what is unscientific have been made reasonably clear, I think.

PHAEDRUS: Yes, I thought so; but remind me
again how.

SOCRATES: You need to know the truth of each
of the things you speak or write about, and be

capable of defining the whole thing by itself; having defined it, you then need to know how to chop it up again into its forms, until you come to what cannot be chopped up; you need to distinguish the nature of soul according to the same principles, discover the form which is in tune with each nature, and in this way plan and order your speaking, to a complex soul offering complex speeches using all the modes, and to a straightforward soul straightforward speeches. Only then will it be possible for you to handle speech-making in a scientific way, so far as its nature allows, or make any attempt at instruction or persuasion, as the whole of our argument so far has made clear.

PHAEDRUS: Yes, that certainly was pretty much how it came across.

SOCRATES: And then what about whether it's right or wrong to deliver and write speeches? And what manner of doing so could, or could not, justifiably be called a disgrace? Haven't the things we've just been saying made it clear...

PHAEDRUS: Made what clear?

SOCRATES: That if Lysias or anyone else has ever written, or ever will write, either in private life or public life – proposing legislation, and hence writing a political work – and thinks his speech contains anything much in the way of validity or clarity, then this kind of writing is a disgrace to the writer, whether or not anyone admits it. Ignorance, waking or sleeping, of what is just and unjust, what is bad and good, cannot avoid being called a disgrace, even if the common run of people approve of it.

PHAEDRUS: No, it can't.

SOCRATES: The alternative is to believe that a written speech on any particular topic is bound to contain a great deal which is purely by way of entertainment; that nothing worth taking very seriously has yet been written, in verse or prose – or indeed spoken, as rhapsodes speak their works, without any questions or explanations, aiming only to persuade; that the best written speeches have 278 really acted as a reminder to those who know; that it is only in teaching, in things which are spoken by way of education and truly written in the soul concerning what is just, what is fine and what is good, that what is clear and complete and worth taking seriously is to be found; that speeches of this kind should be spoken of as if they were the writer's own legitimate sons – first and foremost the speech within him, if it is to be found there, and after that any of its offspring or brothers which have b meanwhile come into existence, as you'd expect, in the differing souls of differing men; and that we can say goodbye to speech of any other kind. The man who thinks like this, Phaedrus, is likely to be the sort of man whom you and I might pray that we should both come to be.

PHAEDRUS: Well, I for one certainly hope and pray for the things you describe.

SOCRATES: In that case, let's call a halt to our entertainment on the subject of speech-making. What you must do is go and tell Lysias that the two of us have been down to the spring and home of the Nymphs, and been listening to speeches with a c message for Lysias and anyone else who composes speeches, for Homer and anyone else again who has composed verses, plain or sung, and for Solon and anyone whose works are composed in the shape of political speeches, under the name of laws. The message is this: if these compositions are based on a knowledge of the truth, an ability to defend them when he comes under attack for what he has written, and the power to show by his spoken words that what he has written is of little account, then he should not take his name from those written works, and be called by that, but from the things he has been truly serious about.

d

PHAEDRUS: What names do you give him, then?

SOCRATES: To call him wise, Phaedrus, in my opinion at least, is too much; only a god can be wise. Lover of wisdom, or something like that, would be more appropriate, and more seemly.

PHAEDRUS: And certainly quite justified.

SOCRATES: On the other hand, those who have nothing of greater value than their works or writings, who spend ages turning them upside down, cutting and pasting – these I imagine you will be justified in calling poets, or speech-writers, or the drafters of laws, won't you?

e

PHAEDRUS: Unquestionably.

SOCRATES: Then that is what you must tell your friend.

PHAEDRUS: And what about you? What are you going to do? It's important not to forget about your friend, either.

SOCRATES: What friend is that?

PHAEDRUS: The fair Isocrates. What message will you have for him, Socrates? And what are we going to call him?

SOCRATES: Isocrates is still young, Phaedrus.
279   But I'd like to give you my prediction for him.

PHAEDRUS: What do you predict?

SOCRATES: I think he is superior, in natural talent, to Lysias and his speeches; and what is more,
that he has a nobler admixture of elements in his
character. It wouldn't be at all surprising, as he gets
older, if the very speeches he is working on now
didn't set him apart, as a man among boys, from
anyone who has yet turned his hand to speech-
writing. And if that is not enough for him, he may
be led on by some more inspired prompting to still
greater things. There is some kind of natural gift for
b   philosophy in that man's mind, my friend. That is
my message from the gods of this place to Isocrates,
as if I were his lover. The other you must take to
Lysias, as if you were his lover.

PHAEDRUS: It shall be done. And now let us go,
now that the heat has become less intense.

SOCRATES: Shouldn't we say a prayer to the gods
here before we go?

PHAEDRUS: Of course.

SOCRATES: Dear Pan, and all other gods of this
place, grant that I may become good in my heart.
May my external possessions not be at war with
c   what is within. Let me regard the wise man as rich.
And let my store of gold be no more than a man of
moderation can pick up and carry away.

Have we left anything out, Phaedrus? For me,
that is a reasonable prayer.

PHAEDRUS: Make it a prayer for me too. The
fortunes of friends cannot be divided.

SOCRATES: Let us go.

NOTES

Symposium

172 (Prologue) The *Symposium* is narrated by Apollodorus, who owes his own knowledge of the event to an earlier narrative by Aristodemus. This elaborate framing structure serves to distance the event from the reader, and may carry the implication that some at least of the narrative is fictitious. Certainly there has been selectivity, as is explicit at 178a and 180c, where Aristodemus' faulty memory is blamed.

174b 'Let's ignore the proverb...' In this paragraph we see how the cultivated Athenians of Plato's day made use of quotations and allusions to well-known literary texts, above all the Homeric epics, to illustrate a point or clinch an argument. Homer in particular was central to the Greeks' literary culture. The 'proverb' comes from Homer's contemporary Hesiod (fragment 264). Menelaus as 'a man of straw' alludes to an insulting reference to him by an opponent in *Iliad* 17.587–8; Agamemnon's hospitality comes from *Iliad* 2.408. The phrase translated here 'Two heads are better than one' is also Homeric (*Iliad* 10.224).

177a '*Melanippe*'. The phrase 'This account is not my own, I had it from my mother' was a famous tag from Euripides' play 'Melanippe the Wise' (fragment 484 K). In the speech which followed Melanippe expounded a philosophic doctrine which may well have seemed incongruous in a young woman's mouth.

177b Prodicus was one of the sophists who taught rhetoric and other intellectual techniques to interested clients. He appears in Plato's *Protagoras*, where he is something of a figure of fun. His works do not survive.

Sophists and others often turned their hands to frivolous or paradoxical subjects such as praising trivia or exalting unattractive subjects. The eulogy of salt referred to is one such composition. Another surviving work in the same vein is Gorgias' defence of Helen, in which he argues that the notorious adulteress was free of responsibility for her actions.

177d 'love is the only thing I ever claim...' This is picked up later, at 198d, where Socrates claims to know the truth about love. In a number of dialogues

Socrates presents himself as an expert on love, because he is regularly infatuated with attractive young men. But here his 'knowledge' is deeper and less
sensual than such passages normally suggest.

178b 'Hesiod'. The reference is to *Theogony* 116–22.
       'Parmenides'. Fragment B13 Diels-Kranz.

178e–9a The Sacred Band of Thebes was an army of this type, but was
probably not yet in existence when Plato was writing: it was established in
378 B.C.

179b 'Homer says . . .' *Iliad* 10.482–3, and elsewhere.
       'Alcestis'. The story of how she sacrificed herself to save her husband
Admetus is dramatized by Euripides in his play *Alcestis*. In that version
Heracles wrestles with Death and recovers her. Phaedrus gives the story a
different twist, to suit his argument.

179d 'Orpheus'. A mythical singer and musician whose playing was said to
charm even the wild beasts of the mountains. His wife Eurydice, according
to the later account by Virgil, died of snakebite; Orpheus descended to the
underworld and nearly succeeded in recovering her, but looked back at the
last moment, breaking the condition set. The story of a phantom suggests a
different version, and indeed early authors varied as to whether Orpheus
succeeded or not.

179e 'Achilles'. The hero of the *Iliad*, who stops at nothing to avenge his
dear friend Patroclus. In Homer the two are not portrayed as lovers, but the
version of Aeschylus in his play the *Myrmidons* evidently made much of
their physical relationship. Phaedrus is right that Homer makes Achilles the
younger man (*Iliad* 11.786–7). On the age-relation between lovers in Plato's
Athens see Introduction, p. xviii.

180d Pausanias is distinguishing two different goddesses on the basis of
differing genealogies found in the poets. In Hesiod Aphrodite was born
from the genitals of Uranus (the Sky), whereas in Homer she is the daughter
of Zeus and Dione. The myths included many variants of this type.

182b 'they are complex'. Pausanias' speech has often been taken as a docu-
ment of social anthropology, but it should be clear that he is simplifying and
schematizing for the sake of his argument; in reality the distinctions between
different Greek states would be less clear-cut. It is also clear that there is a
jocular side to his speech: see esp. 182b 'when they're such poor speakers'.

182c 'Tyrants here in Athens'. Pausanias is referring to the assassination of Hipparchus, one of the sons of the tyrant Pisistratus, by the two lovers Harmodius and Aristogeiton in 514 B.C. This arose from an insult to Harmodius by Hipparchus, who had been spurned by him. The assassination was a botched job (the other brother, Hippias, continued to rule as tyrant for several years), but Athenian folk-memory celebrated the two brothers as romantic liberators of Athens.

183e 'spreads his wings and is off'. Homer, *Iliad* 2.71.

186e 'Asclepius'. Mythical son of Apollo, a gifted healer who was regarded as the founder of the medical profession.

187a 'Heraclitus'. An early philosopher from Ephesus in Asia Minor (c. 500 B.C.). This is fragment B51, but it is widely agreed that Eryximachus misinterprets it; certainly he is unduly patronizing about Heraclitus!

189c 'a rather different kind of speech'. Aristophanes' speech is suitably humorous, with a fantastic, fable-like narrative and a strong emphasis on matters sexual. This suits his frivolous outlook as a comic poet, and although many moderns have found his account of the 'divided' nature of humanity moving and impressive, it is likely that Plato is satirizing him to some extent.

190b 'the giants'. The story of how they piled Mt Pelion on Mt Ossa is referred to by Homer, *Odyssey* 11.307–20.

193a 'like the Arcadians by the Spartans'. This is a mischievous (and anachronistic) reference to the Spartans' destruction of the walls of the Arcadian city Mantinea in 385 B.C. (see Xenophon, *Hellenica* 5.2.5–7). The inhabitants were dispersed to four settlements elsewhere, removing a threat to Spartan hegemony.

193b 'Pausanias and Agathon'. These two had a long-standing relationship, also alluded to at 177d.

195a 'to work systematically through the subject'. Agathon proceeds to do so, following what is evidently already a standard sequence for a speech in praise of someone (the Greek word being 'encomium'). Agathon covers the birth of Eros, his external appearance, and his virtues, including justice, modesty, courage and wisdom (four cardinal virtues). Piety, another standard virtue, is omitted, as Eros is himself a god. Formal rhetorical encomia contemporary with Plato include Xenophon's *Agesilaus*, which has a similar well-organized structure.

195b 'Birds of a feather'. Homer, *Odyssey* 17.217–18.

195c 'cutting, or tying, each other up'. Agathon refers delicately to the myths of brutal warfare among the gods in earliest times: Cronos was said to have castrated his father Uranus, and Zeus imprisoned the Titans in Tartarus. See also 197b. In the *Republic* Socrates strongly criticizes these stories as blasphemous and immoral.

195d 'goes upon the heads of men'. Homer, *Iliad* 19.92–4.

196c–d 'hold his ground'. Sophocles, *Thyestes* fragment 256 Radt.

197e 'in part fun, in part ... serious'. This seems to echo the conclusion of Gorgias' whimsical Defence of Helen. Agathon's ornate, poetic style and rhetorical presentation of his material are both reminiscent of Gorgias, as Socrates remarks.

198c 'The speech reminded me of Gorgias...' Gorgias was one of the most distinguished of the sophists, famous for his teaching of rhetoric and for his poetical prose style. Socrates jokingly combines a reference to this contemporary figure and an allusion to Homer's *Odyssey* (11. 633–5), where Odysseus, interrogating the ghosts at the edge of the underworld, is afraid that Persephone may send up the head of the Gorgon and turn him to stone.

Plato regularly represents Socrates as critical of rhetoric and its practitioners: see Introduction, p. xxi. This is more prominent in the *Phaedrus*, and of course in the *Gorgias*, in which Socrates challenges Gorgias himself.

199a 'My tongue promised, not my heart'. A notorious phrase from Euripides' *Hippolytus* (line 612).

201d 'Diotima, from Mantinea'. Plato's Socrates regularly ascribes his knowledge to outside sources (e.g. *Meno* 81a), and it is likely that Diotima, of whom we do not hear outside this dialogue, is a fictitious figure. The name means 'honoured by Zeus' or 'honouring Zeus'; Mantinea is apt because of the similarity to the Greek word *mantis* ('prophet').

202d 'a great spirit'. In the *Symposium* Plato makes Eros an intermediate being, a spirit or daimon, whereas in the *Phaedrus* he makes him a god. Exact doctrinal consistency is not his aim.

203a 'Who are his parents?' The story which follows may well be Plato's own invention. Contrast the more traditional references to stories of Eros' origins in the earlier speeches.

203d 'in the open street'. In several respects Socrates and Eros are alike: Socrates too is poor, barefoot, hardy, fond of the beautiful. This ingenious analogy can be pursued by considering Alcibiades' comments on the gap between Socrates' unprepossessing appearance and the beauty and wisdom he conceals within his ugly exterior (216d–17a).

208d 'Codrus'. A mythical king of early Athens. The story was that the Dorians invaded Attica during his reign, having been given an oracle that they would be victorious if they spared Codrus. The king tricked them into killing him by disguising himself as a woodcutter, and so saved his country for his heirs.

212d 'Alcibiades'. A noble and beautiful but unprincipled aristocrat, one of the most colourful figures of the late fifth century. His scandalous career, during which he changed sides several times, was a significant factor in arousing Athenian hostility against Socrates, who was thought to have encouraged his unpatriotic behaviour. These views are referred to by Xenophon in his *Recollections of Socrates* (i.1–2). Xenophon attempts to rebut them, but Plato uses the closing scenes of the *Symposium* to show what he saw as the true relations between Socrates and Alcibiades.

214b 'a doctor is worth a dozen ordinary men'. Homer, *Iliad* 11.514–15.

215a 'using similes'. This practice seems to have been a regular Athenian party game: compare Aristophanes, *Wasps* 1308ff.; Plato, *Meno* 80.

215b The aged Silenus was the drunken companion and mentor of the wine-god Dionysus, while the satyrs, half-men and half-goats, were a band of revellers who, together with the female Maenads, followed the god on his journeys. The satyrs in particular were generally portrayed as ugly and lustful. Socrates' appearance seems to have been unusual enough to be caricatured in this way. Marsyas was one of the satyrs, notorious for seeking to rival Apollo on the pipes and being flayed for his offence. Olympus is another mythical musician, often associated with Marsyas.

215e 'Pericles'. Thought by many (including the historian Thucydides) to be the ablest of Athens' political leaders during the second half of the fifth century. His powers as an orator were acclaimed by others besides Plato: e.g. the comic poet Eupolis declared that he was the only one of the orators who left his sting after you heard him speak.

216b 'the Sirens'. In Homer's *Odyssey* (12.154–200), the Sirens seek to lure Odysseus with their songs to sail closer to them and wreck his ship on the rocks. He escapes because he has made his men deafen themselves with wax and tie him to the mast so that he can listen without being able to do as the Sirens want.

219a 'like Diomedes'. In Homer, *Iliad* 6.232–6, Glaucus and Diomedes swear friendship and exchange armour, but as Glaucus' armour is gold and Diomedes' is bronze, Homer comments that Diomedes has got the better of the deal.

219e 'Potidaea'. A subject of Athens which revolted in summer 432 B.C. An Athenian force defeated Potidaean and Corinthian troops and subsequently laid siege to the city, which finally surrendered in 430. Socrates and Alcibiades were presumably involved in the initial campaign.

220c 'But there's another exploit of this "conquering hero"...' Alcibiades quotes from Homer, *Odyssey* 4.240–3, where Menelaus and Helen are reminiscing about Odysseus' deeds at Troy.

220e 'Delium'. The Boeotians defeated the Athenians near Delium in SE Boeotia in late 424 B.C. Laches was an Athenian general who appears in another Platonic dialogue named after him, in which he expresses enthusiastic admiration of Socrates' conduct on campaign.

221b '...staring at all around him'. A quotation from Aristophanes' play about Socrates, the *Clouds* (line 362).

221c 'Brasidas'. An outstandingly able and daring Spartan general prominent in the Peloponnesian war in the 420s until killed at the battle of Amphipolis in 422.

Phaedrus

227a 'Lysias'. A distinguished orator, over thirty of whose speeches survive, almost all composed for others to deliver in the lawcourts. This was a regular practice, though viewed with suspicion in some quarters: compare 257c, where Phaedrus refers to people who sneer at Lysias, calling him a 'speechwriter'.

'Acumenus'. He was the father of Eryximachus, the doctor who appears in the *Symposium*. Both he and Herodicus (d below) were physicians.

227b 'in Pindar's phrase'. The quotation is from Pindar's first Isthmian ode.

Pindar was the greatest of the Greek lyric poets, composing in the first half of the fifth century.

229b 'Boreas ... Oreithyia'. According to the myth, Boreas, god of the north wind, swept away the Athenian princess Oreithyia to be his bride. These fanciful tales were often subjected to rationalizing interpretations in the fifth and fourth centuries: the historians Hecataeus and Herodotus already practised the kind of demythologizing tactics which Socrates mockingly imitates in what follows.

230e 'Very well. Listen.' It is disputed whether this is an authentic speech of Lysias or a deliberate Platonic parody of his plain and rather matter-of-fact style; the latter is more likely. As Socrates subsequently complains, the speech is weak on structure, with points following one another in no very obvious sequence; it also takes a very low view of what love is like and how lovers normally behave.

235c 'from the fair Sappho ...' Sappho and Anacreon are lyric poets of the archaic period, early and late 6th century B.C. respectively: both were famous for their passionate love poetry, now surviving only in tantalizing fragments. The introduction of poets as sources for Socrates' insights paves the way for the 'inspiration' that enlivens his speeches: similarly he ascribes his second speech to the lyric poet Stesichorus (244a). All of this sets his speech making apart from the prosaic and worldly Lysias.

236c 'quote your own words back at you'. Phaedrus alludes to Socrates' teasing remark at 228a–b. But along with the banter, there is a serious theme, of the intimacy of Socrates and Phaedrus and their knowledge of themselves (cf. 229c) and of each other.

236d 'give ear unto my words'. Another Pindaric quotation (fragment 105 Snell-Maehler).

237a 'I'll speak with my head covered.' This is more than mere clowning by Socrates: it dramatically emphasizes how uneasy he is about speaking on this theme: contrast the way he delivers his second long speech, the recantation (243b 'bareheaded').

'Come, ye Muses ...' The opening of Socrates' speech, with its invocation of the goddesses who preside over the arts, is deliberately high-flown; by contrast the second paragraph descends to a story-telling, fable-like style. The contrast is peculiar, and may be meant to indicate Socrates' inner conflict: as yet he is only partly 'inspired', and he is not happy with the task he has been set. In the event, his speech here is better-composed than Lysias', goes deeper into the potential help and harm that a relationship can provide, and importantly brings up the crucial topics of the soul, wisdom and philosophy.

'clear-voiced ... Ligurians'. There is an untranslatable pun, as *ligus* in Greek means 'clear'. The etymology is whimsical.

'Take up with me'. Probably a poetic quotation, but unidentifiable.

238c 'nymph-possessed'. It was thought that possession of this kind might occur in lonely or deserted spots. But Socrates' reference is hardly serious, and his adoption of a more solemn and poetic tone is surely his own initiative.

238d 'dithyrambic'. Dithyramb was a form of religious song in honour of Dionysus. Surviving samples are scarce, but there seems to have been a tendency to use long and elaborate compound words, creating a highly artificial poetic style.

239b The concept of philosophy, in the sense of moral self-improvement, is introduced for the first time. Compare 241c on 'the development of his soul'.

241d 'As wolf loves lamb...' In the Greek this last sentence is almost a full hexameter line: as this was the metre of epic poetry such as Homer's, Socrates comments that he has gone beyond dithyramb to epic (e).

242b 'greatest originator of speeches'. Besides the present occasion, Plato may mean us to think of the *Symposium*, where it was Phaedrus' original proposal that began the series of speeches on love. It is not clear why Simmias (a character in the *Phaedo*) is also mentioned: possibly because the theme of that dialogue, the immortality of the soul, will also be important in Socrates' main speech here.

'that strange spiritual experience'. This seems to be a feature which goes back to the original Socrates (it also figures in Xenophon's works about him). He believed he had occasional warnings or signals from some divine source, which invariably warned him not to do something he might have been about to do. Here the experience is put to effective dramatic use, shifting the dialogue on to a new track.

242c–d 'in Ibycus' words...' Ibycus was one of the lyric poets of the later sixth century B.C. This is one of a number of fragments from his works, now lost (fragment 310 Page).

242d 'a god'. Cf. note on *Symposium* 202d.

243a–b Tradition held that Homer was blind, though this may originate in the portrayal of blind bards in his poetry. The story about Stesichorus is probably an invention of Plato's, but it presumably rests on his having composed two different treatments of Helen, one of which is quoted here (fragment 192 Page). These lines became famous, partly through the popularity of the *Phaedrus*.

Helen, according to the usual version, was seduced by Paris and left her husband Menelaus to journey to Troy, whereupon the Greeks launched their punitive expedition to recover her. In his 'Palinode' or recantation Stesichorus appears to have narrated a version which made Paris carry off a phantom Helen, while the real one, innocent of adultery, lived on elsewhere. The Stesichorean treatment is lost, but the idea was developed by Euripides in his *Helen*.

243c 'brought up on the waterfront'. We see something of the classical Greek aristocrat's prejudices against the navy: armed warfare on land, or cavalry, was thought to be a higher form of military activity.

244c These etymologies are inaccurate, and are certainly not meant to be taken seriously by Plato. Word-play and joke-etymologies are frequent in the dialogues (compare 237a), often frivolous but sometimes hinting at a deeper truth. Plato devotes a whole dialogue to discussion of far-fetched etymologies (the *Cratylus*).

244d 'long-standing guilt'. Plato is thinking of mythical characters such as Orestes, who was persecuted by the Furies, or in rationalizing terms went mad because of his crime in killing his mother. Madness was also, however, closely allied in the Greek mind with prophecy and inspiration (compare Cassandra in Euripides' *Trojan Women*).

246e 'Hestia'. She naturally remains at home, being the goddess of the hearth.

247c 'nectar to drink'. Reminiscent of scenes in the *Iliad* when the gods return to Olympus from expeditions to the world of mortals (esp. 5.368–9).

248c 'in some wild beast'. Having argued that the soul is immortal, Socrates now outlines a process of reincarnation in successive forms, animal and human, with a hierarchy of merit among the souls. Ideas of reincarnation as animals were promulgated by Pythagoras, who had much influence on Plato's thought. The principle of periodic reincarnation appears in several of Plato's myths, especially that at the end of book 10 of the *Republic*, and some of what is said there may be presupposed here.

249a 'come up for judgment'. The idea of punishment in Hades, at least for major wrongdoers, goes back to Homer; Plato and others develop it further, sometimes with harrowing detail. It figures also in the *Gorgias*, *Phaedo* and *Republic*.

249b 'each chooses the life it wants'. This passage in particular seems to presuppose the fuller account in the myth of book 10 of the *Republic*: see 617d–20d.

249c 'recollection'. The idea that the soul can recall the truth of reality which it has at one time 'seen' in its disembodied state is a recurrent one in Plato, explored in different ways in the *Meno*, the *Phaedo* and here.

252b 'Some of the Homeric school'. There was a group or guild in classical times who were known as 'the Sons of Homer' (Homeridae) and claimed expertise on his poetry. Already at this date there were questions raised about the authenticity of some of the works attributed to Homer, and about the variant versions of the text; the Homeridae may have set themselves up as arbitrators. The lines quoted are clearly made up by Socrates, although he is drawing on an idea which is certainly present in Homer, that the gods and men have different names for certain things (e.g. *Iliad* 1.402ff., 2.813–40).

252c 'Ares'. The war-god, hence the violence of the reaction described. Yet this is at odds with Plato's usual argument that the gods are good and that no evil qualities should be ascribed to them.

255b 'Zeus'. Most of Zeus' mythical affairs concerned mortal women, but he was also enchanted by the beauty of the Trojan boy Ganymede, whom he carried off to Olympus to be his cup-bearer.

256a–e This is a central passage on the topic of 'Platonic love' (see Introduction, p. xvii). As will be seen, Plato's conception does not altogether correspond to modern usage. Here the emphasis falls on self-discipline, in the *Symposium* on transcendence of the physical.

256c 'though less so than the other pair'. The paradox of Lysias' speech (that one should yield to a non-lover rather than a lover) is superseded by the even stranger paradox that lovers are closer to one another, and more truly friends, if they do not make love in the physical sense.

256d 'the journey beneath the earth'. This element is not clearly explained, though it figures more prominently in the myth of the *Phaedo* – another sign that the reader of the *Phaedrus* is expected to bring some previous knowledge of Plato to this dialogue.

257a 'somewhat poetical'. Compare 233c, echoed here. Phaedrus' poetic taste is also illustrated by his speech in the *Symposium* (178aff.), which is rich in quotations and references to the myths.

257b 'his brother Polemarchus'. Polemarchus is a lively participant in the discussion dramatized in the *Republic*, book 1.

'pursuit of wisdom'. This is the clearest indication that the *Phaedrus* is in large part a dialogue about the choice of one's proper path in life – and specifically, the choice of Phaedrus between slick but superficial rhetoric as practised by Lysias, and philosophic enquiry as represented by Socrates. It is open to dispute how far Phaedrus in fact responds to this challenge. A similar choice faces the young and talented Isocrates: see 278e, with note there.

257c–d 'speech-writer'. Oratory was admired but also treated with suspicion by many Athenians, not least the older conservative types who may have thought that Aristophanes had got it right in describing it as the art of turning the worse cause into the better. Although unskilled speakers who were forced into court might well have to make use of a professional speech-writer in order to make their defence effective, they would often try to conceal the fact that they had done so (it is common for defendants in the Athenian courts to represent themselves as speaking without sophistication, depending on the unadorned truth).

258c Lycurgus (?7th century B.C.), an almost mythical figure, was the great lawgiver of Sparta, as Solon (flor. *c.* 590 B.C.), a much more vivid historical personality, was at Athens. Darius was King of Persia from 522 to 486 B.C. Although not a legislator in the same sense, he did much to tighten up the administration of the Persian empire.

259b 'Sirens'. See note to *Symposium* 216b.

'Something I've never heard of, I suspect.' In fact the story of the cicadas is very likely to be Plato's own invention, though it draws on story-patterns which are common in Greek mythology: metamorphosis, enchantment by magical female powers, servants reporting human behaviour to higher deities. Again the poetical tale is suited to Phaedrus, described here as 'a lover of the Muses' (compare 257b).

259c 'They tell Terpsichore...' This seems to be the earliest passage assigning specific provinces to the particular Muses, though it is true that some of their names, including Terpsichore's (she who delights in the dance) already give strong indications of their field of interest.

259e–60a 'not in the truth'. It was commonly complained that orators were indifferent to the facts provided they won their case. Phaedrus' comment that what the orator needs is to be able to discern the jurors' opinion highlights the difference between rhetoric as commonly practised (by Gorgias, Lysias and others) and rhetoric as it should be. Socrates proceeds with a critique of the ignorance of the orator: his art is not really a science, merely a form of cheating. There are connections here with the *Gorgias*, the earlier dialogue in which Socrates fiercely criticizes contemporary oratory in the political sphere.

260a 'loath to cast away the speech'. A quotation from Homer, *Iliad* 2.361.

260e 'not a science, simply a knack'. This phrase seems to be a reference to the fuller argument of this point in the *Gorgias* (see 463b, 501a).

261b 'Nestor ... Odysseus ... Palamedes'. Heroes of the Trojan war. Both Nestor and Odysseus were famous, especially in Homer, for their powers as speakers; Palamedes was also a highly intelligent Greek hero who was supposed to have invented a number of techniques, including counting and dice! 'The man's a Palamedes' was a way of praising cleverness (e.g. Aristophanes, *Frogs* 1451). The notion that they might have written textbooks on rhetoric is evidently absurd, but Socrates is parodying the widely-held view that Homer enshrined all forms of knowledge, including rhetoric. In fact the Homeric poems have many fine examples of rhetorical practice, but theory was a later development.

261c 'Thrasymachus ... Theodorus'. Contemporary sophists and theorists.

261d 'Palamedes who comes from Elea'. Socrates means the philosopher Zeno, a significant figure of the early fifth century, whose paradoxical arguments intrigued Plato and many others since. He was a pupil and friend of Parmenides, and appears in Plato's dialogue named after the latter.

264a 'light of my life'. This translates a high-flown phrase from Homer's *Iliad* (8.281 and elsewhere).

264c 'any speech should be like an animal'. The principle that a work of oratory, and any work of art, should be in some sense organic, a harmonious whole, was taken up by Aristotle in the *Poetics* and has had lasting influence. Compare further 268c–d. It has often been observed that we cannot easily see the *Phaedrus* itself as meeting this standard: whether this is deliberate on Plato's part, and if so why, are much-debated questions.

'Midas, king of Phrygia'. A legendary figure most famous for the story of his 'golden touch'. The verses quoted also survive in a slightly longer version, ascribed to a poet called Cleoboulos of Lindos: they are probably not composed by Plato, but may nevertheless be only a literary invention, rather than a genuine epitaph.

266b 'techniques of dividing and bringing together'. The preceding passage has outlined two general techniques of argument, collection and division, which are prominent in Plato's later works, notably in the *Sophist* and the *Statesman*. Their importance in this dialogue seems more incidental.

'close behind I follow ...' An adaptation of Homeric phrases: compare esp. *Odyssey* 5.192–3.

'dialecticians'. Experts in dialectic, that is in philosophic argument through dialogue.

266c 'Thrasymachus and the rest ...' The sophists, who among their other interests all seem to have taught rhetoric, and many of whom, Thrasymachus included, wrote textbooks on the techniques of oratory. In the next few pages Socrates makes fun of the elaborate range of technical terms which these books had introduced, and refers to various sophists by name. These works are lost, though we know something about some of them from Aristotle's *Rhetoric* and other sources.

267c 'our doughty hero from Chalcedon'. Thrasymachus.

269a 'honey-tongued Adrastus'. King of Argos and leader of the Seven against Thebes. The phrase is similar but not identical to an expression in the early elegiac poet Tyrtaeus (fragment 12 West). Pindar refers to an oration Adrastus made at the funeral of the other heroes on that expedition, and Euripides develops this hint in his play the *Suppliant Women*. In the next sentence Socrates shifts to a historical example, the Athenian statesman Pericles (see note on *Symposium* 215e).

270a 'windbaggery and stargazing'. Anaxagoras (*c.* 500–428) was a major figure among the pre-Socratic thinkers, who asserted the fundamental homogeneity of reality but also the infinite variety of appearances. Pericles was generally thought to be an intellectual, and seems to have associated with several literary and artistic contemporaries, including the sophist Protagoras. But, as the translation suggests, Socrates' tone is ironic: we are not meant to suppose that he believes Pericles had real philosophic knowledge.

In the *Phaedo* Socrates describes the disappointment he himself felt on reading Anaxagoras' work (97b–99c).

270c 'Hippocrates'. The most famous doctor of antiquity, *c.* 469–*c.* 399 B.C. Numerous writings survive under his name (including the original 'Hippocratic oath'), but many if not all of them are later works and it is hard to reconstruct him as a historical figure. Asclepius was the mythical prototype of the physician, also referred to at *Symposium* 186e.

273a 'Tisias'. Pupil of Corax, and usually paired with him. Both were Sicilian rhetoricians, who appear to have taught how to make the improbable seem probable. Tisias was already mentioned in the satirical treatment of textbooks at 267a.

273c 'whatever he is proud to take his name from'. This jokingly alludes to the name of Corax (see last note), which in Greek means 'crow'.

274c 'What I heard was this.' As with the tale of the cicadas, this story or myth was probably invented by Plato, though the names of Thamus, Ammon and Theuth are authentic enough. The Greeks were fascinated by Egypt, with which they had contacts from early times (in the *Odyssey* Menelaus and Helen journey there on their return voyage from Troy), and it was widely believed that some important parts of Greek culture derived from the much older Egyptian civilization. The second book of Herodotus' History is a massive survey of Egypt, including much fact and fantasy.

Naucratis was a Greek settlement founded in Egypt (on the East bank of the Canopic branch of the Nile) in the seventh century B.C., important especially for trade.

275b 'At the temple of Zeus...' Dodona was said to be the oldest Greek oracle. The responses were allegedly delivered through the rustling of the leaves of Zeus' sacred oak tree. Socrates means that Phaedrus' scepticism is over-sophisticated: rather than questioning Socrates' source, he should look for the lesson implicit in the tale. This passage complements the comments of Socrates on the 'clumsy rationalism' of the demythologizers (229d–30a). Socrates by contrast is prepared to learn from myth and indeed compose his own. The phrase 'listen to oak and rock' wittily uses in literal terms an enigmatic metaphor found in early poetry (e.g. *Iliad* 22.126–8).

276b 'sow them in midsummer, in window-boxes'. This alludes to the so-called 'gardens of Adonis'. Adonis was a beautiful youth beloved by Aphrodite, but was slain by a boar, in some versions sent by a jealous Ares. The Athenians held a festival, particularly celebrated by women, in lamentation for Adonis. The ritual involved sowing seed at midsummer in broken pots and placing them on rooftops: the seeds were naturally shortlived. Hence the 'gardens of Adonis' are proverbially swift to wither and die.

276d 'age of forgetfulness'. Probably a poetic quotation, but untraced.

277e 'nothing worth taking very seriously has yet been written'. It is obviously paradoxical that this comment is made in a written dialogue (though one which mimics the to-and-fro of actual conversation). This passage has been much quoted, but often over-interpreted: Plato does not deny all value to writing in general, still less deprive his own work of any significance: what he does do is emphasize that wisdom must be found by the individual, and internalized, written in his soul, not accepted blindly from books.

278e 'the fair Isocrates'. A new character is unexpectedly introduced. Isocrates (436–338 B.C.), a gifted Athenian, son of a rich man and pupil of a number of the sophists, began as a speech-writer like Lysias but became a more ambitious teacher of political rhetoric and (at least in his own mind) of statesmanship. Large portions of his writings, including pamphlets on his own methods and principles, still survive. Whatever the original Socrates may have thought of him, Plato was critical; Isocrates makes a number of hostile references to Plato's Academy, and may have seen himself as a rival educator. The references to his potential for philosophy are surely ironic, with an added edge because Isocrates attempted to hijack the term and apply it to his own teachings.

ABOUT THE TRANSLATOR

TOM GRIFFITH was Head of Classics at Marlborough College, Wiltshire. He is General Editor of Wordsworth's Classics of World Literature series and has recently translated *The Republic* for Cambridge University Press.

ABOUT THE INTRODUCER

DR RICHARD RUTHERFORD is Tutor in Greek and Latin Literature at Christ Church, Oxford. His books include *The Meditations of Marcus Aurelius: a Study* and *The Art of Plato.*